AWESOME
Human Body Science Experiments
for Kids

AWESOME HUMAN BODY SCIENCE EXPERIMENTS for Kids

40 STEAM PROJECTS TO EXPLORE HOW THE BODY WORKS

ORLENA KEREK, MD

WITH GALEN AND DANTE KEREK

Illustrations by Kate Francis

ROCKRIDGE PRESS

First Rockridge Press trade paperback edition 2022

Rockridge Press and the Rockridge Press logo are trademarks or registered trademarks of Callisto Media Inc. and/or its affiliates in the United States and other countries and may not be used without written permission.

For general information on our other products and services, please contact our Customer Care Department within the United States at (866) 744-2665, or outside the United States at (510) 253-0500.

Paperback ISBN: 978-1-68539-273-4 | eBook ISBN: 978-1-68539-509-4

Manufactured in the United States of America

Series Designer: Katy Brown
Interior and Cover Designer: Richard Tapp
Art Producer: Megan Baggott
Editor: Maxine Marshall
Production Editor: Melissa Edeburn
Production Manager: Lanore Colopriso

Illustrations © 2022 Kate Francis. Photography © 2022 Evi Abeler, cover.
All other images used under license © Shutterstock.
Author photo courtesy of Cristina Quílez.

10 9 8 7 6 5 4 3 2 1 0

To Carlton, Galen, Dante,
Celeste, and Sebastian.
Our amazing family.
We love you all.

CONTENTS

PART III

PUTTING IT ALL TOGETHER

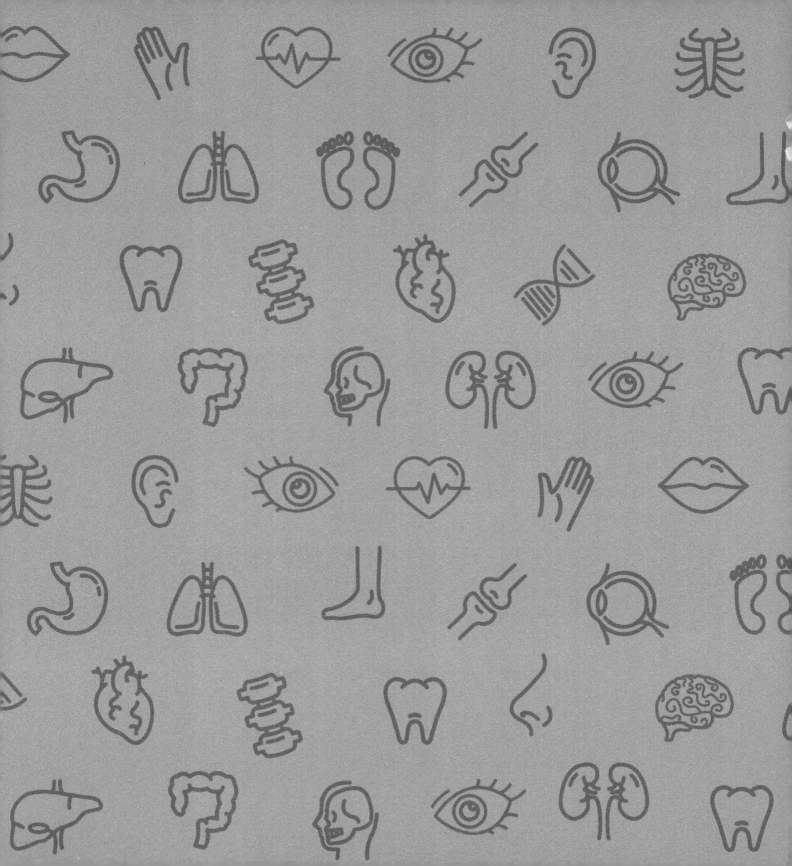

INTRODUCTION

The human body is one of the most amazing things on this planet. Are you ready to learn all about it? In this book, you'll find 40 fun activities that explore how your body and its systems work.

If you are reading this book, I bet you love to get your hands dirty by doing activities and experiments. I love that, too! When you do hands-on activities, you get to see things in action, rather than just read about them. That's the spirit of 🅢 🆃 🅔 🅐 🅜. STEAM stands for **SCIENCE**, Technology, **ENGINEERING**, Art, and Math. All these subjects are about being creative and learning at the same time.

My name is Dr. Orlena, and I'm excited to share this book's activities with you. I'd also like to introduce two of my children, Galen and Dante, who helped me write this book. They've given these activities their "fun seal of approval," making sure I didn't include anything boring! Both Galen's and Dante's names are inspired by famous thinkers. Galen is named after Galen of Pergamon, who practiced medicine 2,000 years ago. Galen of Pergamon discovered the body's pulse, which is something you'll learn about in one of our activities. He also thought that putting blood-sucking animals called leeches on your body would cure you of lots of things. Yuck! Luckily, doctors have discovered much more since then. Let's start discovering, too!

THE AMAZING HUMAN BODY

Discovery through STEAM is all about asking questions. It took many people asking a lot of questions to discover how the human body works. Remember Galen of Pergamon? When he was alive, people didn't have the tools we have now. Nevertheless, Galen discovered about blood and how it moves through our bodies. Just like anyone learning anything new, he considered many wrong ideas to find some right ones. For example, he thought that blood was made in the liver. Do you know where it's actually made? If not, that's okay. You'll find out soon!

Thanks to the hard work of scientists and other experts in Ⓢ Ⓣ Ⓔ Ⓐ Ⓜ, we now know (mostly) how the body works. And now you're going to learn, too! Are you ready?

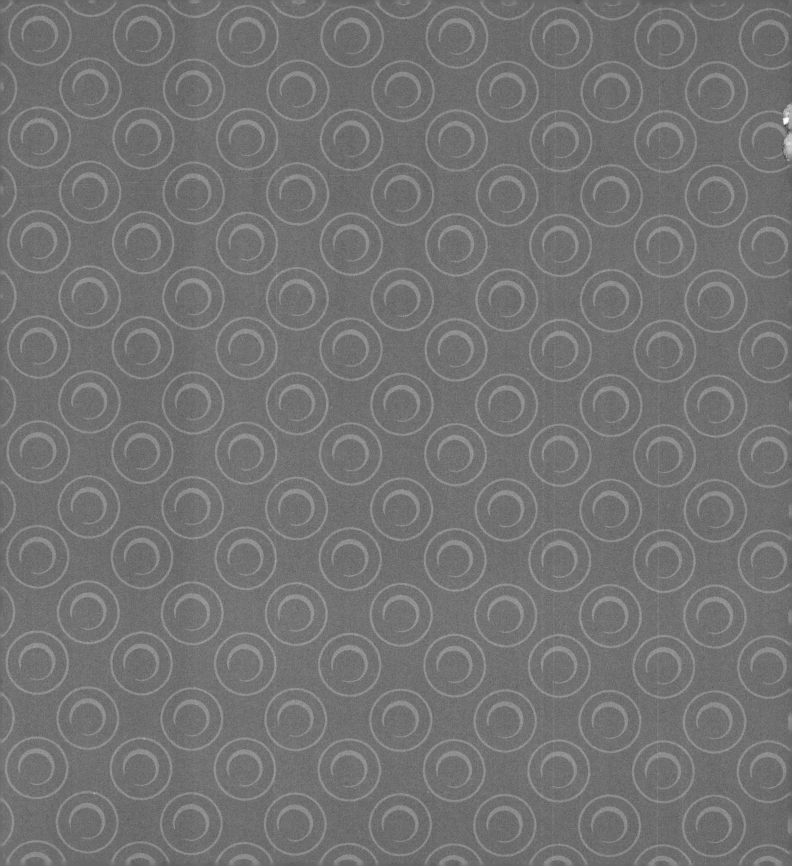

Chapter 1

ALL ABOUT THE HUMAN BODY

What is your body made of? How do its parts work together? Let's discover the answers to these questions so that you are prepared for the experiments that come later in the book. In this chapter, you'll explore **ANATOMY** and **PHYSIOLOGY**, which will help you understand how the different parts of your body fit together. You will also find out the jobs that each body part does to help you move, think, eat, and more.

SO, WHAT IS A BODY?

Every living thing has a body. When you look in the mirror, you can see your face. Your face is part of your body. Your body has lots of other parts you can see, too, like your hands, arms, legs, and feet.

Your body also has stuff on the inside that you can't see in the mirror—for example, your brain and heart. Some things in your body, like your blood cells, are so small you can't see them without a special machine called a **MICROSCOPE**. Inside and out, the big and little parts of your body work together to build **you**.

Your body helps you do so many amazing things! It can help you eat your food, play games, use a wheelchair, talk with friends, read this book, and so much more.

Human bodies come in many shapes and sizes. Some are tall, some are short. People have different colors of skin and hair. We all have different abilities. Even so, our bodies work the same! We all have the same tiny things (like cells) and big things (like organs), which work together to build systems. Let's take a closer look at the human body.

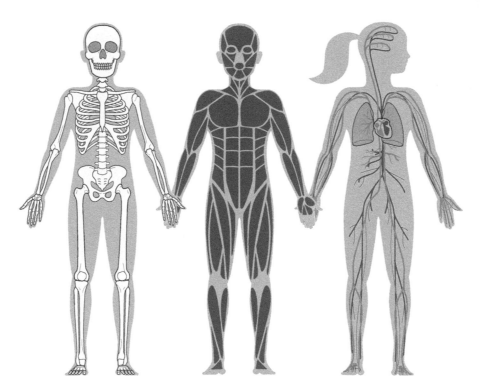

AWESOME HUMAN BODY SCIENCE EXPERIMENTS FOR KIDS

CELLS

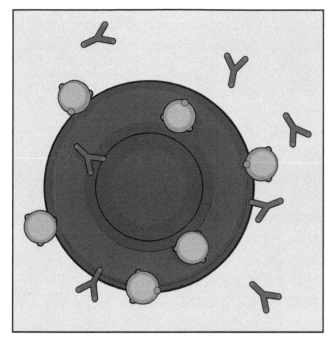

*Red blood cells carry oxygen
to all parts of the body.*

CELLS are the smallest parts of our bodies. You can think of them as bricks in a building. Many tiny cells are stacked up to build our bodies, just like many small bricks stacked to make a tall building.

Our bodies have trillions of cells. A trillion is a million million! That's a number so large it is hard to imagine. Have you ever been to a beach? When you pick up a handful of sand, you are holding around 10,000 grains of sand. A sandcastle might be made up of two million grains of sand. To reach a trillion grains of sand, you'd need to fill half a million buckets. That's a lot of sand—and a lot of cells!

The trillions of cells in your body are of 200 types. These types are like bricks with different colors and shapes. Together, these cells combine to form tissues.

There are four main types of cells: connective tissue cells, nerve cells, muscle cells, and epithelial (skin) cells.

Connective tissue cells include cells like blood cells. Blood cells help deliver energy and oxygen to other cells. Blood cells also clear the waste from our bodies and protect us from illnesses. Bone cells are also connective tissue cells. They build bones that hold our body together and protect our organs. Some bone cells have

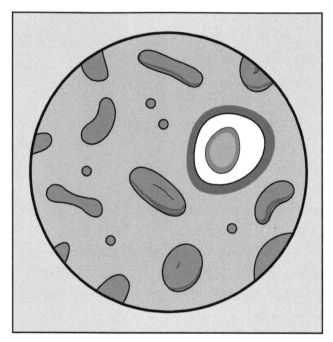

Our bodies contain more than 200 different types of cells. Red and white blood cells are connective tissue cells.

another important job. On the inside of our bones is our bone marrow, which makes red blood cells.

Nerve cells include special cells in the brain called NEURONS. They have many jobs to do, including thinking and making sure your entire body is working! You're using your brain cells right now to read this book.

Guess where you can find **muscle cells**? In your muscles, of course! There are three types of muscle cells. Skeletal muscle cells occur in the muscles attached to your skeleton. These cells are shaped like little tubes. Cardiac muscle cells are found in your heart. Smooth muscle cells are found in your digestive system. The main function of all these cells is to make movement.

There are different types of **skin cells**. They are divided into layers on your skin. The top layer is called the epidermis. The middle layer is called the dermis. The bottom layer is called the hypodermis. Our skin has many functions that you're about to learn about.

LET'S TALK ABOUT TISSUES

There are four main types of tissue in the human body.

TISSUES are groups of cells that work together to do a job. For example, red blood cells, white blood cells, and plasma cells join to form the tissue we call blood. Blood has lots of jobs. One job is to deliver oxygen. Just like there are four main types of cells, there are also four main types of tissues: connective tissues, epithelial (skin) tissue, muscle tissue, and nervous tissue.

Connective tissue helps hold other tissues together so our bodies don't fall apart! Bones, blood, and **LYMPH** (a clear liquid that flows through our bodies) are all examples of connective tissue.

Epithelial tissue is made up of thin layers of cells. Skin is a tissue that covers the outside of our bodies. It stops unwanted things from getting into our bodies and stops the stuff we want inside our bodies from falling out. There are other types of epithelial tissues, too, like the tissue that lines your stomach.

Muscle tissues help us move. We have **MUSCLES** all over our bodies, like the muscles in our arms and legs that help us walk and play. Our hearts are made of muscle tissue that pumps blood around inside our body. Luckily our heart muscles don't get tired, like our arm and leg muscles do!

Nervous tissues help carry messages from our brains to different parts in our body. If you want to move your arms and legs, your brain sends a signal along the nervous tissue to activate the muscle tissue.

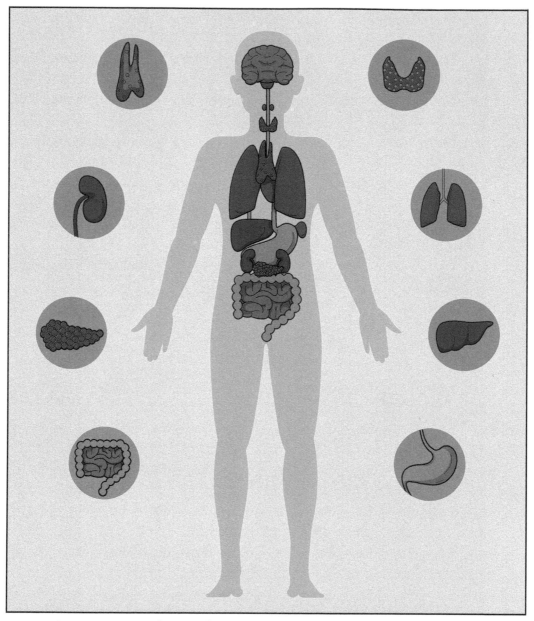

Organs are made up of tissues that work together. Each organ in the body has a special shape which helps it do a specific job.

AWESOME HUMAN BODY SCIENCE EXPERIMENTS FOR KIDS

THE BODY'S ORGANS

A collection of tissues that work and live together is called an ORGAN. Your heart is an important organ that pumps blood around inside your body.

Your **brain** is an organ, too! The brain sits in your head and does plenty of thinking. The brain figures things out and makes sure all the other parts of the body are doing their jobs properly. Did you know your brain is made of mostly water and fat? It is surrounded by fluid, which helps protect it when you bump your head.

Your **stomach** is an organ that helps break down food. After you swallow your food, it travels to your stomach. Your stomach is like a big mixing machine. It mixes the food with chemicals that start to break it down into a liquid called chyme.

Here are some organs you may not have heard of:

Our **kidneys** help filter out things we don't want from our blood. They also make sure we have the right amount of water in our bodies.

Our **liver** also helps get rid of things we don't want. It cleans our blood by getting rid of harmful chemicals called toxins. The liver also helps us digest food by creating a liquid called bile, which breaks down fats that we eat.

Our **spleen** is an organ in our ABDOMEN. It sits to the left of our stomach. The spleen helps protect us from germs.

Our **pancreas** is also in our abdomen, behind our stomach. It helps us get energy from food. The pancreas also makes ENZYMES, which help us digest food and store energy.

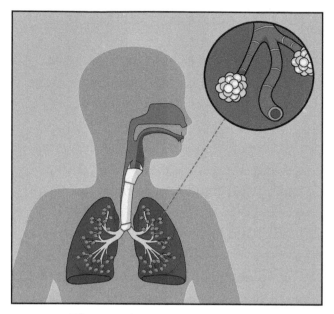

The respiratory system is an organ system in the body.

A group of organs work together to do a complex job. This group is called an **ORGAN SYSTEM**. There are 12 different organ systems in our bodies, including the **DIGESTIVE SYSTEM**, the **CIRCULATORY SYSTEM**, and the **RESPIRATORY SYSTEM**. We will explore these systems through activities later in the book. First, let's take a closer look at the respiratory system to help us understand how organ systems work.

Our respiratory system allows us to breathe in fresh air containing oxygen. Our cells need oxygen to help us use energy from our food. So, the respiratory system does a very important job. It also helps us get rid of carbon dioxide, which is a gas that we don't want to build up in our bodies. The respiratory system lets us talk and sing, too!

The main organ in our respiratory system is our lungs. This system also includes our nose, mouth, and trachea. The trachea is a tube that connects the nose and mouth to our lungs. Bones called ribs protect our lungs and help them move in and out when we breathe. Our lungs are a bit like a sponge. You can squeeze water out of a sponge, but the sponge can't do it by itself. Our lungs need muscles to pull the air in and out.

When you breathe, your respiratory system is at work! Air travels in through your mouth or nose, down the trachea, and

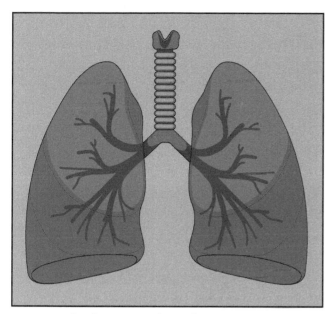

The lungs and trachea are part of the respiratory system.

into the lungs until it reaches a small part of the lungs called the alveoli. The alveoli is where the oxygen from the air enters our bloodstream. The carbon dioxide that we don't want in our blood passes back through the lungs, up through the pipes, and out our nose or mouth. We repeat this cycle all the time.

Thanks to the respiratory system, we now have oxygen in our blood. That's great, but oxygen still needs to go where it's needed: inside our cells. Do you remember how many cells we have? Lots and lots! The oxygen travels around in our bodies by way of our red blood cells. We use our circulatory system to get the oxygen to all those cells. The circulatory system includes our heart, arteries, veins, and blood.

All the systems in our bodies use many different cells, tissues, and organs to do important jobs. These systems are also connected to each other. For example, the respiratory system provides the oxygen that the circulatory system carries around the body.

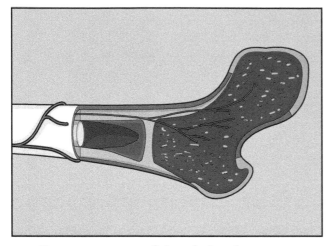

Bones are part of the skeletal system.

We move our bodies using the **SKELETAL SYSTEM**, which is made up of bones, muscles, ligaments, and tendons. Our bones are strong and protect the soft inside parts of our bodies. Our muscles flex and lengthen to move our bones. Ligaments and tendons connect muscles and bones.

Bones also give our bodies structure. Can you think of any animals that don't have bones? Picture a worm or a jellyfish. Their bodies are soft and floppy because they don't have any bones.

We have bones in different shapes and sizes. Some are big and some are very small. Our biggest bone is the thigh bone in your leg, which is also called the femur. Your smallest bones are in your ears. The tiniest one is called stapes, and it looks like a stirrup. Your stapes is smaller than a pea!

Our bones aren't solid all the way through. If they were, they'd be really heavy! Instead, our bones have a honeycomb-like center called bone marrow. It's the **BONE MARROW** that makes most of our blood. That means our bones help us move **and** make blood. How amazing is that?

Some bones hardly move at all. For example, our skull is made of different bones that are stuck together, protecting our brains. Some other bones are connected by

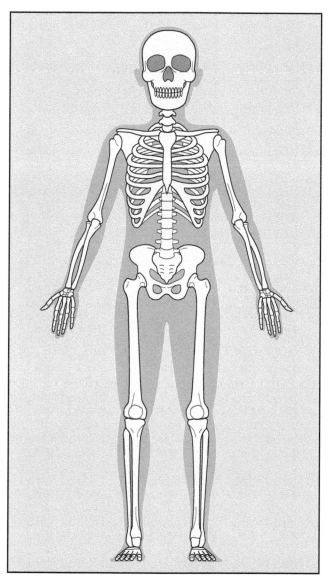

Joints are places where bones connect to each other. Can you spot all the joints in this picture?

JOINTS. There are different types of joints in our bodies. They allow our bodies to move, bend, and twist in different ways. Think about how an arm moves through space. The arm can rotate at the shoulder, bend at the elbow, and bend at the wrist.

The most common type of joint in the body is called a synovial joint. These joints have a special fluid in them. This fluid makes it easy for the bones to move against each other. Synovial joints come in different shapes that allow different movements. A hinge joint allows only two movements, like opening and closing a door. When you bend your knee, you're using a hinge joint. Other joints, like a pivot joint, allow different turning movements. Your neck is a pivot joint.

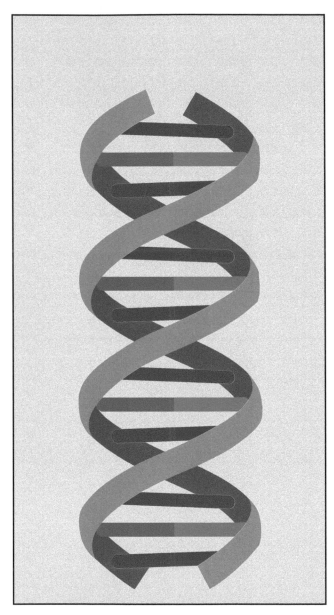

DNA is made of chemical elements like nitrogen. DNA is stored in every cell in the body.

Our bodies are made up of many different **CHEMICAL ELEMENTS**. On page 5, we imagined that cells were like the bricks that make up a tall building. If you looked very closely at a brick, you would see that it's made of tiny grains of sand and rock. Chemical elements are like those grains. They are even smaller than cells! There are 60 different chemical elements in the body.

Most of our body is made up of four elements: oxygen, carbon, hydrogen, and nitrogen. More than half your body is water, which is a combination of the elements oxygen and hydrogen.

Carbon is an element that builds most of life on planet Earth! It combines with hydrogen and other elements to form strings of elements called compounds. Our planet is a carbon-based planet, meaning all living things are made up of different carbon compounds. Yes, every living thing, including trees, plants, and animals. And you!

Nitrogen is needed to make our muscles, hair, nails, skin, and blood. Nitrogen is also important to make our **DNA**. Have you heard of DNA? It's like a computer program that tells your body what cells to make.

Calcium and phosphorus are two other elements in our bodies. We need both of them for healthy bones and teeth. They have other important jobs, too, like making sure our heart beats properly.

THE HUMAN BODY AND STEAM

Our bodies are incredible and very complicated. Because there are so many systems inside the body, it has taken hundreds and hundreds of years to understand how they work. Before we invented machines and other cool technology to help us learn, people had to watch the body closely and guess what was happening. Sometimes they got it right, and sometimes they didn't.

Even a long time ago, people performed operations to heal sick people. As far back as 3000 BCE, people used to cut holes in skulls to relieve the pressure inside. This medical procedure is called trephining, and doctors still do it today.

Over the centuries, people have used all aspects of science, technology, engineering, art, and math to figure out how the body works. Have you heard of Leonardo da Vinci? He used art as a useful tool for learning by making detailed drawings of the insides of bodies.

People have built on and expanded what other people have learned. Now we understand a lot about the human body. We also understand more about how things outside the body affect us. For example, people in the past didn't know what germs were. They didn't know that something as simple as washing our hands can stop us from becoming unwell.

Using science, technology, engineering, art, and math, people have invented new ways of keeping us safe. Vaccinations help protect us from diseases. We have amazing tools like X-ray machines to let us see what is happening inside our bodies.

You're going to use STEAM to learn about the human body, how it all fits together, and how it works. Get ready for an amazing adventure!

Chapter 2

HOW TO USE THIS BOOK

Now that you've read about how the body works, it's time to see it in action. You're going to use your body to find out about your body! The activities in this chapter will connect everything you learn with the fields of Ⓢ Ⓣ Ⓔ Ⓐ Ⓜ.

The activities are ordered from easiest to hardest. The simplest activities are at the beginning, and they gradually increase in difficulty. This book is yours, so you can do the activities in any order you like. Feel free to skip around and do the ones that look most fun to you.

GETTING READY

Each activity is labeled so you can see how easy or difficult it is. There are 12 easy activities, 16 medium activities, and 12 challenging activities. Some activities have a caution sign. Make sure you follow the safety instructions carefully to get the most fun out of the activity.

Let's get going! Where are you going to start? Do you want to find out what a pulse is and what happens to your pulse when you run around? How about making a model of your lungs? Or squashing up strawberries so you can extract DNA, like a real scientist? It's up to you! There is so much to learn about your body and STEAM.

DOING THE PROJECTS

Once you have chosen which activity you'd like to do, start by reading every step. Make sure you collect all the materials you'll need before you begin. Doing so will help you get the results you want and save you from disappointment.

Most of the materials are items you can find around your home, like tap water, an empty glass, or a rubber band. There are some materials you might need to get from your local store. They're all inexpensive items that should be easy to find, like a balloon or food coloring.

When you read the activity, you will find pictures with the step-by-step instructions. The images are there to help you follow the steps and know you're doing them correctly.

Some of the activities can be done all by yourself. Even so, it's important to tell an adult what you're up to, so be sure to get their permission before you start any activity. Sometimes you might need them to lend you a hand!

The "Hows and Whys" section that follows each activity explains everything that happened. There are also STEAM connections so you can understand how the activity fits into the world of science, technology, engineering, art, and math. Finally, the Try This! section will help you get creative if you'd like to change the activity or try it again.

Learning about the human body includes learning lots of new words. Did you know that when doctors are training, they learn 15,000 new words? If you find a word you don't know, check out the Glossary at the back of the book. The Glossary is a list of important words to help you boost your STEAM knowledge.

DOS AND DON'TS

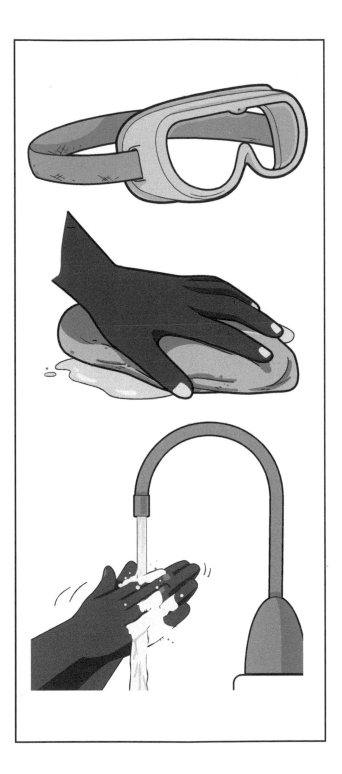

DO

1. Follow the instructions!

2. Ask permission from the adults looking after you before you start an activity.

3. Invite other people to do the activities with you and talk about what you've learned.

4. Have fun!

5. Practice safety first! Messy activities have a caution note with their instructions. Consider wearing goggles to protect your eyes for any messy activity.

DON'T

1. Play around with sharp objects, like scissors.

2. Worry about mistakes! Mistakes are great. They are how you learn. When something doesn't work, think about why it didn't work and then try again.

3. Leave your mess lying around. Clean your hands and your work area after each activity, and carefully dispose any leftover material.

Part II

THE EXPERIMENTS

It's action time! Let's dive into some awesome experiments! Here, you'll find activities to explore how the sense of taste and smell are connected, how the heart pumps blood, how skin keeps our insides safe, and so much more! Remember, if your activity doesn't work out the first time, you can try again. That's what people in ⓢⓣⓔⓐⓜ do! If your project doesn't look like the picture, that's okay, too. The point is to have fun and see what you can learn. Don't forget that the activities start out simple and get more complicated later on in the book. You can do the activities in any order you like, so pick the one that sounds most fascinating to you in the moment.

SWEET AND SOUR

DIFFICULTY LEVEL: EASY

TIME: 20 MINUTES

MATERIALS

- Sweet fruit, like berries, melon, apple, or orange
- Notebook
- Pencil
- Milk chocolate
- Water

 Have you ever wondered how we taste food? Our mouths have **PAPILLAE**, or taste buds, that taste different flavors. The papillae are mostly on the tongue, but there are also some on the roof of your mouth and in your throat. The things we eat and drink can affect how other foods taste. How does that work? Let's find out!

STEPS

1. Take a bite of your fruit. In your notebook, write down how sweet it tastes on a scale of from 1 to 10, with 1 being not sweet at all and 10 as the sweetest thing you've ever tasted.

2. Next, eat a piece of chocolate. Note how sweet it is on a scale of from 1 to 10.

3. After scoring the sweetness of the chocolate, take another bite of fruit. Does it taste the same as before? If not, is it sweeter now, or less so? Does it taste acidic or sour? Write your **OBSERVATIONS** in your notebook.

4. Repeat the experiment, but this time have a mouthful of water between each bite. Make any notes about how drinking the water changes the flavor of the fruit and chocolate.

MATERIALS

HOWS & WHYS: Fruit contains naturally occurring sugar. Chocolate also has sugar, but it's added sugar and there's much more of it. When we eat lots of sugar or salt, our taste buds get used to those strong flavors, making mild flavors harder for our taste buds to notice.

STEAM CONNECTION: Scientists do experiments to test how different things impact each other. Here, you are using experimentation to discover how different foods affect the taste of each other and your taste buds.

Try This! Try eating different foods and see how they affect the taste of the fruit. What happens if you eat a slice of lemon instead of a piece of chocolate? Remember to note your findings and observations in your notebook!

MAKE YOUR MARK

DIFFICULTY LEVEL: EASY
TIME: 15 MINUTES

MATERIALS

- Stamp ink pad
- Uninflated balloon

 Look at your fingertips very closely. Can you see wavy lines across them? These are ridges in your skin. They create different patterns that we call fingerprints. Do you have the same fingerprints as your friends and family?

STEPS

1. Press the pad of your thumb onto the stamp pad to cover your thumbprint with ink.

2. Now press your thumb onto the balloon to create an ink print of your thumb. Be careful not to smudge the print when you pull your thumb away.

3. Next, blow up the balloon so it is big and full of air. Don't let it pop! You can tie off the end of the balloon, or just pinch it closed with your fingers so the air doesn't leak out.

4. Look at the place where you pressed your thumb onto the balloon. What do you see?

5. Try pressing your other fingers and other people's fingers onto the balloon. Look carefully at the the fingerprints and thumbprints. Do you see a difference in the patterns?

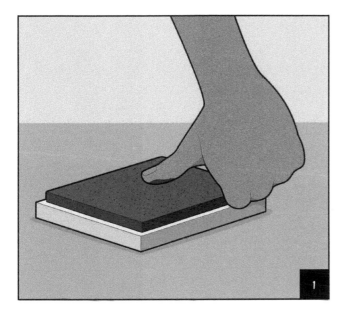

HOWS & WHYS: All fingerprints are different. You won't have the same fingerprints as anyone else, not even if you have a twin. Your fingerprints formed before you were born. When babies are first developing, their fingers don't have fingerprints. Then, the skin starts to create grooves and ridges, which are impacted by what the unborn baby touches in its surroundings.

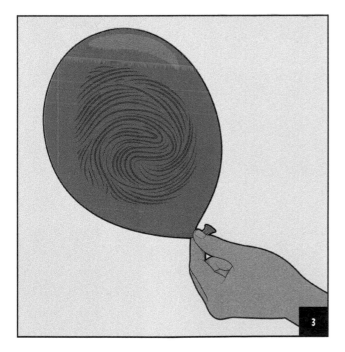

STEAM CONNECTION: Artists sometimes create imprints or tracings. They etch an image into wood or metal, cover it with ink or paint, then transfer it onto paper to create a picture. You are using a similar technique here to observe the patterns in your fingerprints.

Try This! Try touching your fingers to different things to see if they leave a fingerprint. What happens if you put your fingers on a clean glass?

MAKE A MODEL

DIFFICULTY LEVEL: EASY

TIME: 10 MINUTES

MATERIALS

➲ Red modeling clay

 Our bodies need oxygen to survive. Red blood cells carry oxygen around inside our body. These cells work like little delivery trucks that bring oxygen to all the parts that need it. Let's make a model of a red blood cell to see how it works.

STEPS

1. Roll a lump of clay into a ball. Imagine you are rolling a tiny snowball.

2. Place your index finger on one side of the ball and your thumb on the other side. When they are in place, gently push your two fingers closer together. (If your fingers meet, you've gone too far!)

3. Your clay should look like a ring doughnut without a hole in the middle. This special shape is called a **BICONCAVE DISC**.

HOWS & WHYS: Red blood cells deliver oxygen to other cells in our bodies and carry away carbon dioxide. The biconcave disc shape helps them do this job quickly. Their shape also helps them squeeze through tiny blood vessels where other shapes might get stuck.

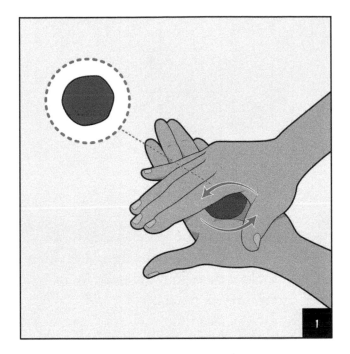

STEAM CONNECTION: In this activity, you are thinking like an engineer. Engineers must think about what the best shape is to do a specific job. Can you imagine what would happen if engineers decided to put square wheels on our cars?

Try This! How many models of red blood cells can you make? Try making several models and see how they stack or fit together. Did you know you have 25 trillion red blood cells in your body? It would take a lot of clay to make that many cells!

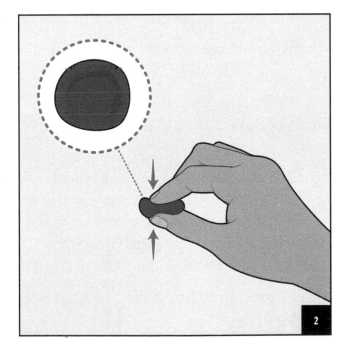

PUPIL POWER

DIFFICULTY LEVEL: EASY

TIME: 15 MINUTES

MATERIALS

- ❯ A partner
- ❯ Notebook
- ❯ Pencil
- ❯ Dark room
- ❯ Stopwatch or phone timer
- ❯ Small flashlight

 The black circle in the center of your eyes is called the **PUPIL**. The pupil lets light into your eye to help you see. Have you ever noticed that your pupils can get bigger or smaller? Let's discover what affects the size of your pupils.

STEPS

1. Look at your partner's eyes. Pay special attention to the size of their pupils. How big or small does the black circle look? Your partner should look at your eyes, too. Write down your observations in your notebook.

2. Go into the dark room with your partner, or turn off the lights in the room you are in. Set your timer for 5 minutes and wait.

3. Come back into the well-lit room or turn all the lights back on.

4. Look at the size of each other's pupils. Do you notice a difference from before going into the dark room? Write down your observations in your notebook.

5. Shine a flashlight into your partner's eyes. Do it quickly and gently because the bright light may irritate the person it is being shone at. It won't damage their eyes, but they might not enjoy it. Do you see the size of the pupil changing? Write down your observations in your notebook.

6. Shine the flashlight carefully in one of their eyes but look at the other eye. What happens?

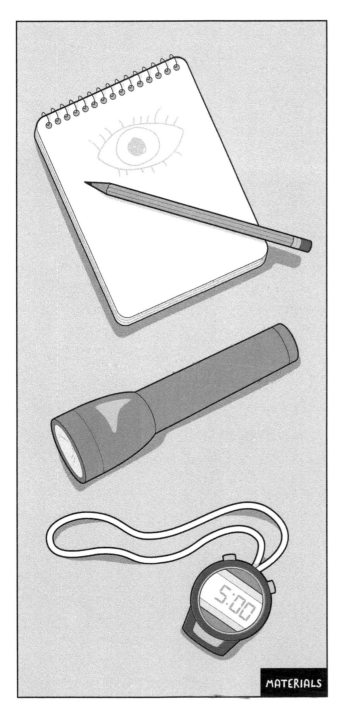

MATERIALS

7. Now go to a place with lots of light, or outside into the sun. Remember to never look directly at the sun. It is bright enough to damage your eyes. Look at each other's eyes again.

HOWS & WHYS: The colored part around your pupil is the **IRIS**. It is a muscle that helps your pupil get bigger or smaller. When you go into a dark room, your pupils get bigger, or dilate, allowing more light to enter your eye. When you go into a lighter room, your pupils get smaller, or constrict, to let in less light.

STEAM CONNECTION: Cameras use a technology that is similar to your pupils. It is called an aperture. An aperture is a hole that gets bigger or smaller to let in more or less light. If the camera lets in too much light, the details in the picture will be hard to see. If the camera doesn't let in enough light, the picture will be too dark.

Try This! Wear a patch on your eye like a pirate to help your eyes adjust to darkness. The eye that is covered by the patch is always adjusted to darkness. When you go into a dark room, take off the patch. You'll be able to see without needing to wait for your eyes to adjust.

READY, STEADY, PULSE!

MATERIALS

- Stopwatch or phone timer
- Notebook
- Pencil

? When you are playing sports, you might hear a lot about pulse. Your pulse is the beating of your heart throughout your body. You can feel it on your wrist, your chest, or your neck. In this activity, you'll learn about your pulse and how it applies to athletics.

STEPS

1. Find your pulse. Put a finger on the inside of your wrist until you feel a beat. If you can't find it there, press your finger to the side of your neck or press your hand to the left side of your chest.

2. Once you can feel your pulse under your finger or hand, set your timer for 1 minute (60 seconds). While the timer is going, count how many times you feel your heartbeat.

3. Write down the number of beats you felt. Your count will probably be somewhere between 70 and 115.

4. Do some physical activity! Run around, do jumping jacks, play with a jump rope—whatever gets you out of breath. Do this activity for about 5 minutes. It's okay if you need to take a few short breaks.

5. Now, set your timer for 1 minute and count your pulse again. Is there a difference this time? Is it faster or slower?

6. Write your second pulse count next to the first count. Compare the two. Which one is faster? Why do you think that is?

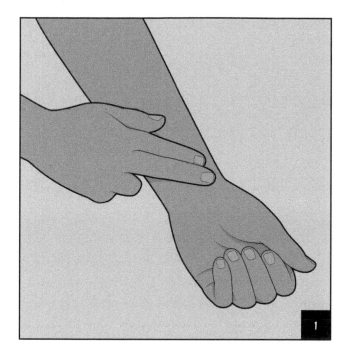

7. Wait 10 minutes so that you can catch your breath and rest. After you have calmed down, count your pulse one final time. Has it gone back down? Do you think its speed has to do with the physical activity you did?

HOWS & WHYS: Your heart is a big, strong muscle that pumps blood around your body. Your pulse is your heartbeat. It speeds up when you are active because the harder you run and play, the more oxygen your muscles need. That means your heart beats faster to get the oxygen pumping into your blood.

STEAM CONNECTION: In math, comparing two numbers means noticing the difference in value. The blood pounding through your arteries created an echo of your heartbeat in your wrist. You're doing basic math by comparing different numbers to see how your pulse changes.

Try This! Do this experiment with a few friends or family members. Record how each of their pulses changes after some physical activity. Is everyone's pulse the same?

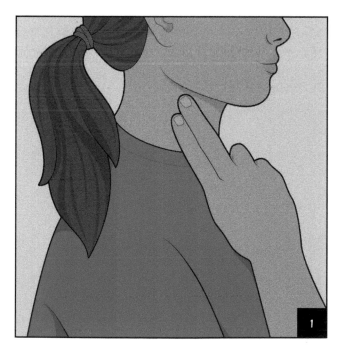

SWEAT IT OUT!

DIFFICULTY LEVEL: EASY
TIME: 10 MINUTES

MATERIALS

- ➔ You!
- ➔ Bath or shower
- ➔ Towel
- ➔ Bathrobe or another dry towel

 When your body gets hot, it makes sweat. In this activity, you're going to add some STEAM to your bath or shower! Doing so will show you how sweat cools your skin down to keep you from getting too hot.

STEPS

1. Take a bath or shower. Make sure your skin is totally wet. Once you are finished, step out of the bath or shower. (Be careful not to slip!) Don't dry yourself yet. Stand still and see how your body feels. Does it feel hot or cold?

2. Stand for a few minutes, or until you start to get cold.

3. Now dry your skin off with a towel. Set the towel aside and focus on how warm or cold your body feels. Do you feel any different now that your skin is dry?

4. Finally, put on your bathrobe or wrap yourself in a dry towel. Notice your body temperature again. Do you feel any different?

HOWS & WHYS: Sweat cools our skin when it **EVAPORATES**. As the water in your sweat turns into vapor, it takes heat away from your body. In this activity, the water on your skin represents sweat. When you dried yourself with a towel, you took the sweat away. Removing the sweat stops the water from evaporating. When you put your bathrobe on, you feel much warmer. Clothes trap warm air around you.

Try This! You don't have to wait until you next have a bath or shower! Run around until you are sweaty, then notice how your body temperature changes as that sweat dries off.

MUSCLE TENSION

DIFFICULTY LEVEL: EASY
TIME: 10 MINUTES

MATERIALS

- Mirror
- Notebook
- Pencil
- Pencil case
- Heavy book
- Full water bottle

 Muscles are the organs in your body that you use to move. You have more than 600 muscles in your body. The muscles help you move around, lift objects, and even keep still. Let's watch our muscles in action!

STEPS

1. Stand in front of the mirror. Roll up your sleeves so you can see your arms. Hold your arms out to the side so they are in line with your shoulders.

2. Now bend your arms at the elbows. As you bend your arms, watch the muscles in your arms. Describe what you see in your notebook.

3. Place your hand on the muscle between your shoulder and elbow. This muscle is called your bicep. Bend and straighten your arm while your hand is still on that muscle. Can you feel how it changes? Write what you feel in your notebook.

4. Keep your hand on your bicep muscle. In the other hand, hold your pencil case. Repeat steps 2 and 3. You are lifting your pencil case like you are lifting a weight. Do you feel anything different in your muscle now that you are lifting some weight? Jot down anything you notice in your notebook.

5. Now swap out the pencil case for the book. Keep your other hand on your bicep to feel your muscle as it moves.

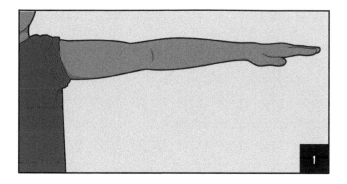

How does it feel compared to the last two times? Write your comparisons in your notebook.

6. Finish off with the water bottle. Ask yourself the same questions as before: What did the muscle feel like?

HOWS & WHYS: The heavier the object, the more your muscle must work. Muscles contract, or get smaller, to create movement. A contracted muscle is in a condition called muscle tension.

STEAM CONNECTION: Engineers create and build things using math and science. When they design something, they have to think about how something will be used and how much tension will be put on it. You created tension when you contracted the muscles in your arms.

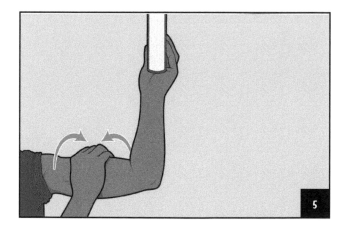

Try This! Repeat this exercise with other muscles in your body. How do you lift your legs? Or move your feet? You don't have to lift things to see what movements make different muscles tense.

SKIN SENSITIVITY

DIFFICULTY LEVEL: EASY
TIME: 15 MINUTES

MATERIALS

- A partner
- Blindfold
- Paper clip
- Sandpaper
- Cotton ball or cotton pad

 Touch is one our five senses. Our sense of touch helps us experience our world. The sense of touch makes it possible for you to feel whether things are hot, cold, rough, or smooth on your skin. This activity explores the sense of touch with a partner. Before touching someone else's body, always make sure you have permission.

STEPS

1. This is a game that you and your partner are going to play. One person is the "feeler" and the other person is the "experimenter." Begin by having the feeler put on the blindfold.

2. Next, the experimenter can choose between the paper clip, the sandpaper, or the cotton ball. Gently press one of these items to bare skin on the feeler's hand, arm, or ankle.

3. The feeler then guesses what touched them and describes how it feels.

4. Repeat steps 2 and 3 with the remaining items.

HOWS & WHYS: Your skin has many thousands of sensors that feel different things, like heat, pain, and pressure. These sensors help us notice when something is hurting us. Areas that touch many things, like your hands, have the most sensors. The large number of sensors makes the hands more sensitive.

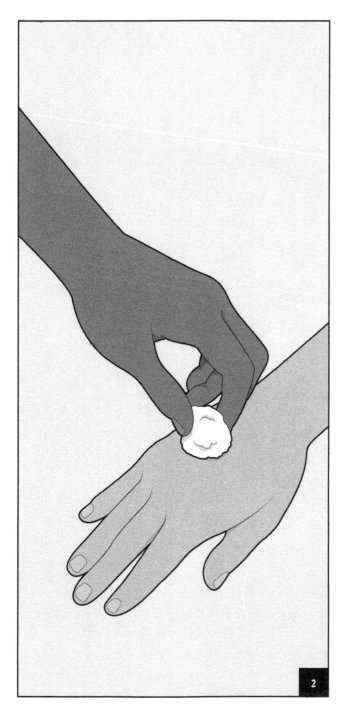

STEAM CONNECTION: Doctors do tests that are similar to the game you played. When they think someone might have damaged their nerves, they check to see if that person can feel in different parts of their body. The doctor touches skin with items like a tuning fork or soft cloth to test sensations like heat, cold, and pain.

Try This! Play the game with a geometry compass. Draw both points of the compass close together. If you touch the compass points to your hand, they might feel like one point rather than two separate points. Instead of guessing what touched you, try to guess how many points the experimenter gently touched you with: one or two?

TASTE TEST

DIFFICULTY LEVEL: EASY

TIME: 30 MINUTES

MATERIALS

- ➔ Paper towels
- ➔ Dry food, like crackers or chips
- ➔ Water

 The spit inside your mouth is called saliva. Saliva is useful for many things! You use saliva to keep your mouth moist and to spit things out of your mouth. Saliva also helps you eat and taste.

STEPS

1. Use clean hands to pat the inside of your mouth with a paper towel. Keep your mouth open for a moment so it stays dry.

2. With your dry mouth, eat a cracker or chip. What do you taste?

3. Drink a small sip of water.

4. Eat another cracker or chip. Does it taste different from your first bite?

5. Repeat steps 3 and 4 until your mouth feels back to normal and is no longer dry. Did you notice a difference in flavor every time you ate a cracker or a chip?

6. Go back and repeat steps 1 and 2. Do you notice more of a difference?

HOWS & WHYS: Normally when you eat, the food mixes with saliva. The food's taste substances dissolve in the saliva, which carries the taste to your taste buds, or papillae. When your mouth is dry without the saliva, the taste substances don't reach the taste buds. You can't taste the food!

MATERIALS

Try This! Do the experiment with different foods. The experience might be different if you eat moist food like a piece of fruit, or sweet food like a piece of candy. Do you notice how your mouth creates more saliva when you eat certain things?

BALANCING IS CHALLENGING

DIFFICULTY LEVEL: EASY
TIME: 20 MINUTES

MATERIALS

- Jump rope
- Notebook
- Pencil
- Stopwatch or phone timer

 How hard is it to stand on one leg? Balance is a difficult skill that many parts of our body help us achieve. Your muscles, your eyes, and even your ears help you when you try to balance!

STEPS

1. Lay the jump rope on the ground, stretched out in a straight line.

2. Try to walk along on the jump rope without falling off. First, try walking normally. Then try walking with your arms stretched out on either side of your body. You can also try running along the rope. Make observations in your notebook. How hard was it to balance on the jump rope? Was it easier with your arms out, or when you were moving faster?

3. Next, try balancing on one leg. How long can you stay on only one leg? Time yourself with a stopwatch. Now try it with your arms out. How long were you able to balance with your arms by your sides compared to how it was with your arms out? Jot down your observations.

4. Balance on one leg again. This time, stare fixedly at one thing that isn't moving, like a blade of grass or a stone on the ground. Does staring at one thing help you stand on one leg longer than if you just look anywhere?

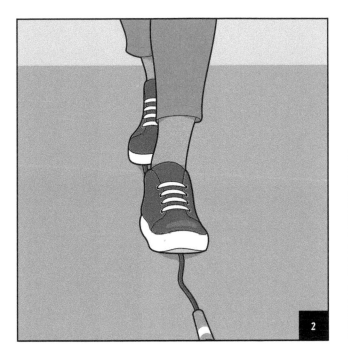

5. Now for the ultimate trial! Stand on the jump rope while balancing on one leg. Try with your arms by your sides, and then stretched out. Try focusing your eyes on one point to help your balance.

HOWS & WHYS: Your inner ear helps you balance by telling your brain where up and down are. The inner ear has three canals, or tubes, that are full of liquid. When your head tilts one way, the liquid sloshes to one side. This sloshing moves tiny hairs in the canals and tells your brain which way is down.

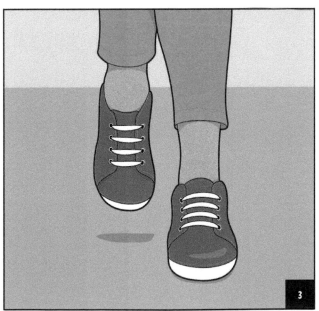

STEAM CONNECTION: Have you seen ballet dancers spin and spin without falling over? They balance by using a technique called spotting. They look at one spot and keep their head still while their body turns. At the last possible moment, they spin their head around and look at the same spot again.

Try This! Try spinning and twirling around without looking at any one spot. What happens? Do you fall over? Now try spotting, like a ballet dancer.

TASTY SMELLS

DIFFICULTY LEVEL: EASY
TIME: 15 MINUTES

MATERIALS

- Blindfold (optional)
- Swimming nose clip (optional)
- Sliced fruit
- Notebook
- Pencil
- Glass of water

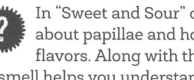 In "Sweet and Sour" on page 22, you learned about papillae and how they can taste different flavors. Along with these taste buds, your sense of smell helps you understand what food tastes like. Check it out!

STEPS

1. Start by putting on the blindfold, if you would like to use one. The blindfold will help you avoid getting distracted by what you are seeing so you can focus on what you are tasting.

2. Hold your nose so you can't breathe through it, or use the swimming nose clip if you have one.

3. Take a bite of fruit with your nose plugged. Write down how flavorful the fruit is, on a scale of from 1 to 10: 1 means you can't taste it at all, and 10 means it is the most flavor you have ever tasted.

4. Take a sip of water to rinse out your mouth.

5. Unplug your nose and eat another bite of fruit. Write down how flavorful the fruit is, on a scale of from 1 to 10.

HOWS & WHYS: Your sense of smell helps you "taste" different flavors. Your brain combines the information from your taste buds and the smell sensors in your nose to understand taste. Without your sense of smell, you can taste only the flavors that your taste buds detect.

MATERIALS

Try This! Try the experiment with chocolate. Do you notice a difference? If not, why do you think that is? Chocolate is so sweet that your taste buds will sense the flavor even with your nose blocked.

THROUGH THE LENS

DIFFICULTY LEVEL: EASY

TIME: 15 MINUTES

MATERIALS

- ◗ Glass jar
- ◗ Water
- ◗ Straw or stick
- ◗ Piece of paper with a drawing or picture on it (like a page from a magazine)

 When people wear glasses, they are wearing lenses. A lens is something that changes the path of light and can make things look bigger or smaller. There are also lenses *inside* your eyes, just in front of your pupils!

STEPS

1. Fill the jar with water.

2. Put the straw or stick into the water. Look at the jar from the side. Does the straw or stick look the same size as it did before?

3. Hold the drawing or picture behind the jar. Look at it through the jar. Does the picture look the same size?

HOWS & WHYS: Light travels in a straight line. But when light hits a lens or the water in the glass jar, it bends and changes direction. The light rays separate, which makes the straw and the picture look bigger. The lenses in our eyes can change shape to help us see things far away or near.

2

3

Try This! Test your eyes by looking at something far away. Now look at something really close, like your fingers. Your eyes are changing focus between the two objects. Is that easy to do?

BREAK IT DOWN

DIFFICULTY: MEDIUM
TIME: 10 MINUTES
(PLUS 3 DAYS OF
OBSERVATION TIME)

MATERIALS

- 2 glass jars, large enough to each fit an egg
- Water
- Laundry detergent without enzymes (like Tide Free and Gentle or All Free Clear)
- Laundry detergent with enzymes (like Arm & Hammer BioEnzyme Power or Tide Hygienic Clean)
- Stick-on labels or tape that you can write on
- 2 raw eggs in the shell
- Notebook
- Pencil

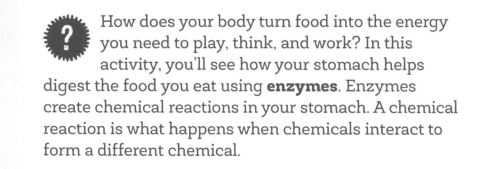 How does your body turn food into the energy you need to play, think, and work? In this activity, you'll see how your stomach helps digest the food you eat using **enzymes**. Enzymes create chemical reactions in your stomach. A chemical reaction is what happens when chemicals interact to form a different chemical.

STEPS

1. Put enough water in each of the jars to cover an egg. Leave some room to add laundry detergent.

2. Stir in 1 tablespoon of detergent without enzymes into one jar, and 1 tablespoon of detergent with enzymes into the other. Label each jar.

3. Put an egg in each of the jars. The water should completely cover the egg so none of the egg is in the air.

4. Every day for three days, check on the eggs. Do so around the same time each day. Are parts of the shell missing? Record what you see in your notebook. You can include any thoughts or ideas about what is happening, too.

5. After three days you should be able to see a big difference. What has happened? Write the results of your experiment in your notebook.

AWESOME HUMAN BODY SCIENCE EXPERIMENTS FOR KIDS

HOWS & WHYS: The egg in the enzyme detergent has much less shell than the other egg. The shell has been broken down by the enzymes. In your stomach, there is a liquid that is very strong acid, which contains enzymes that break down your food.

STEAM CONNECTION: Enzymes help speed up or start chemical reactions. We have lots of different enzymes in our bodies, which do jobs like helping us digest food. People also use enzymes outside the body to do many jobs. Did you know that enzymes are used to make cheese? Cheesemakers use enzymes to help turn milk from a liquid to a solid.

Try This! Leave the egg in the detergent containing enzymes for longer. See how long it takes for the egg to disappear completely, if it ever does. What happens to the water surrounding it? What happens if you put small pieces of eggshell in the water?

THE BIG SQUEEZE

DIFFICULTY LEVEL: MEDIUM
TIME: 10 MINUTES

MATERIALS

- Pair of pantyhose
- Pair of rolled-up socks
- Scissors

 Your stomach is part of the body's digestive system. This system is like a very long tube that goes from your mouth to your bottom. There are special ring-shaped muscles in the walls of the digestive system. The muscles contract in a wave motion to move the food along the tube. This movement is called peristalsis.

 Caution: Sharp scissors should be handled only with adult supervision.

STEPS

1. Cut the foot off the pantyhose to make a long tube.

2. Put the rolled-up socks in one end of the pantyhose tube. They will form a clump inside the pantyhose.

3. Imagine your hand is a ring of muscle. Squeeze the top of the pantyhose. Do the socks move?

4. Squeeze just below where your hand is so the socks go down even more.

5. Continue squeezing until the socks have gone through the hole in the other end.

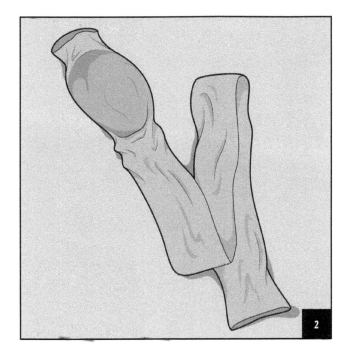

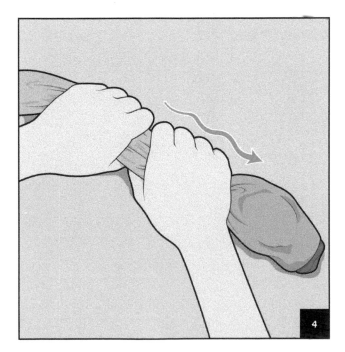

HOWS & WHYS: When you squeeze the pantyhose, the socks may move a little. They don't reach the end of the tube in one go! Similarly, peristalsis works in waves. One section squeezes and moves the food a tiny bit, then the next section squeezes and moves it farther along.

STEAM CONNECTION: Foods like fruits and vegetables contain fiber. When we eat fiber, it sits in the tube of our digestive system. The fiber helps move food along until it passes out of your body in your poop. When you don't eat enough fiber, it is difficult for the food to move along.

Try This! When you get to the end of a tube of toothpaste, notice how difficult it is to squeeze the rest out. That's like your intestines without any fiber. When you open a new toothpaste tube, see how easy it is to come out. You squeeze gently and it comes right out. The new toothpaste tube is like your intestines with lots of fiber in them.

HOW STRONG IS YOUR HAIR?

DIFFICULTY LEVEL: MEDIUM
TIME: 15 MINUTES

MATERIALS

- 1 strand of hair at least 2 inches long. (This strand can be collected from a brush or comb—you don't need to pull out any hair!)
- Pencil
- Sticky tape (optional)
- Paper clip
- Small plastic bag, like a grocery bag
- Small items to use as weights, such as coins or paper clips
- 2 stacks of books that are equal height, or 2 boxes of the same height
- Kitchen scale

Individual hairs look very thin, but they are surprisingly strong thanks to keratin. Keratin is **PROTEIN** that makes up our hair, skin, and nails. In this activity, you're going to see just how much weight your hair can carry.

STEPS

1. Tie the strand of hair to the pencil. If this task is too difficult, you can tape the hair to the pencil. Just make sure you secure it tightly!

2. Tie the other end of the strand of hair to the paper clip. If this task is too difficult, you can tape it on.

3. Hook the paper clip through the top of the plastic bag.

4. Put the two stacks of books or the boxes side by side. Balance the pencil between them. The paper clip with the plastic bag should hang without touching the surface below. If it touches the surface, you can add more books to the stacks or get bigger boxes to make them higher.

5. Add the weights to the bag until the strand of hair breaks.

6. When the strand of hair breaks, put the plastic bag of weights on the scale and see how much it weighs. Does it weigh more or less than you expected?

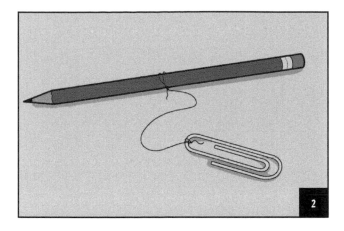

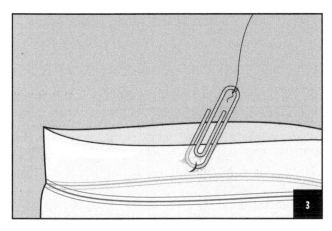

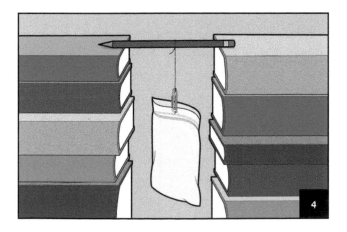

HOWS & WHYS: The protein keratin makes your hair keep its shape instead of breaking. The fibers in keratin stretch easily and can extend a long way before they break.

STEAM CONNECTION: Engineers use similar tests when they want to know how strong things like bridges or buildings will be. They call them stress tests.

Try This! Do the activity with somebody else's hair. What if you try it with curly hair and straight hair? What happens if you take a few hairs and wind them together? If you take 10 hairs and twist them together, can they hold 10 times as much as one hair? Or more?

BENDY BONES

DIFFICULTY LEVEL: MEDIUM
TIME: 30 MINUTES
(PLUS 1 WEEK OF
OBSERVATION TIME)

MATERIALS

- 2 clean, empty glass jars with lids
- 2 clean, cooked chicken bones
- Stick-on labels or sticky tape you can write on
- Marker
- White vinegar
- Water
- Paper towels

? The bones in your body are made of calcium, a chemical element that makes them strong and keeps them from bending. Calcium also helps make your teeth strong! In this activity you will discover what your bones would be like if they didn't have calcium.

STEPS

1. Place one chicken bone in each of the jars. Label each jar. One label should say "water" and the other should say "vinegar."

2. In the jar labeled "water," add enough water to cover the bone. Put the lid on it and set it aside.

3. In the jar labeled "vinegar," add enough vinegar to cover the bone. Put the lid on it and set it aside.

4. Put both jars in a safe place and leave them there for a week.

5. After one week, pour out the vinegar and water.

6. Take the bones out of the jars and carefully dry them with a paper towel.

7. Touch and bend the bones in your hands. What do you see? Do you notice the difference between them?

HOWS & WHYS: The vinegar in the jar dissolves the calcium in the bone. The bone with calcium is strong and rigid. The bone without calcium is bendy and flexible.

STEAM CONNECTION: We get our calcium from foods like milk and cheese, leafy greens, and nuts and seeds. Calcium plays many important roles. Not only does it make your teeth and bones strong, but it also helps your blood clot, your muscles contract, your heart beat, and your nerves work well.

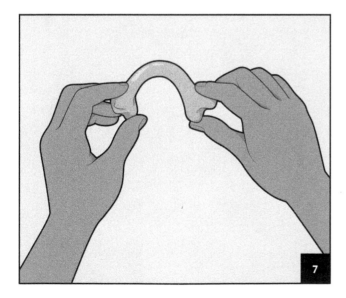

Try This! What jobs are best for a tool that is bendy and flexible? What jobs need something hard and rigid? Take a pool noodle and a long stick. What can you do with both of them? Can you use the stick to carry your school backpack? What happens when you try to carry your backpack with the pool noodle?

SUGARY SHELLS

DIFFICULTY LEVEL: MEDIUM
TIME: 20 MINUTES
(PLUS 2 DAYS
OBSERVATION TIME)

MATERIALS

- 3 raw eggs in the shell
- 3 glass jars with lids
- 1 can of soda
- Lemon juice
- Water
- Notebook
- Pencil

 Why do we brush our teeth every day? Let's use eggs to find out! Eggshells and teeth are both made of calcium and other minerals. So, we can use eggshells to help us understand how things might impact your teeth.

Caution: This experiment involves cooking with heat and requires adult supervision.

STEPS

1. Ask an adult to help you boil the eggs. Once they have cooled, peel off the shells. Set the shells aside to use in the experiment. You can discard (or eat!) the eggs.

2. Pour the soda into one jar, the lemon juice into another jar, and the water into the third jar. Put about the same amount of liquid into each of the jars.

3. Add an eggshell to each jar. Then put the lids on the jars and set them aside.

4. Observe the shells over the next few days. Does anything happen to them? Do the different liquids affect them differently? Why? Write down all your observations and try to draw conclusions from them.

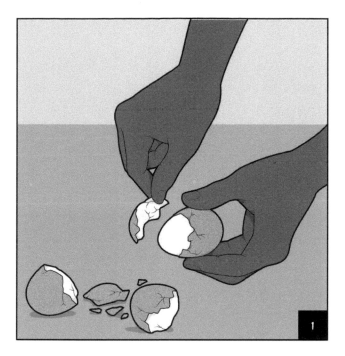

HOWS & WHYS: When you leave calcium (eggshells) in acid (lemon juice), it dissolves. Imagine that calcium was in your teeth. As acid eats away at the calcium in your teeth, it makes holes where bacteria can grow. The bacteria in your mouth make acid by eating sugar and other morsels of food that get stuck in your teeth.

STEAM CONNECTION: Tartar is a material that builds up on your teeth. It has a rough surface, which makes it difficult to clean properly. Bacteria can also hide in the rough patches and damage teeth. Dentists use special tools to clean away tartar so there's fewer places for the bacteria to hide.

Try This! Ask an adult to buy plaque disclosing tablets. The tablets will help you see if you've brushed your teeth well. When you chew the tablet, it'll show where you still have sugar on your teeth by staining them red. Don't worry—you can brush again to remove the color!

ORANGE ARMOR

DIFFICULTY LEVEL: MEDIUM
TIME: 20 MINUTES
(PLUS 2 DAYS OF
OBSERVATION TIME)

MATERIALS

- 8 easy-peel oranges
- Flour
- Salt
- Blue paint (The paint should be runny. If your paint is too thick, add a pea-sized drop of it to a cup of water.)
- Notebook
- Pencil

 In "Skin Sensitivity" on page 36, you saw how your sense of touch helps you feel temperatures and textures. Our skin has other important jobs as well. For example, the skin protects the tissues on the inside of our bodies and keeps out germs and dirt.

 Caution: Don't eat the oranges after the experiment is over! Oranges are very healthy for you, but paint isn't.

STEPS

1. Peel 4 oranges and leave 4 unpeeled. Divide the oranges into pairs. Each pair should have 1 peeled orange and 1 unpeeled orange.

2. Place the flour and salt in piles on a flat surface. Pour some paint onto a plate or into a cup. Add a drop or two of water if your paint is not runny.

3. Roll one pair of oranges in the flour.

4. Dip the second pair of oranges in the blue paint.

5. Roll the third pair of oranges in the salt. Set them aside in a safe place.

6. Set the final pair of oranges next to the salted oranges, to sit in the air.

7. Before you continue, write down what each pair looks like.

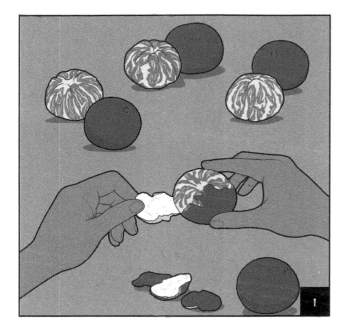

8. Now, look at the oranges in the flour. Does the flour stick to one more than the other? Wipe the flour off and remove the peel of the unpeeled orange. Did any flour get inside the orange? Write down what you observed.

9. Leave the blue oranges for two hours, then remove the peel from the unpeeled orange. Which orange is bluest inside? Write down your observations.

10. Leave the salted pair of oranges and the final pair of oranges for two days. Each day, observe the oranges and write down what you see.

HOWS & WHYS: Just like our skin, the orange peel is a barrier that protects what's inside. The peel prevented the fruit from drying out in the salt and in the air. It also prevented unwanted things from getting inside. That is, without the peel, the flour and paint were able to get inside the fruit. In the experiment, both painted oranges turned blue inside, but the one with the peel was much less blue.

CONTINUED

STEAM CONNECTION: Doctors do lots of things to help people when they get hurt and lose some of their skin. One thing they can do is a skin graft. To make a skin graft, the doctor scrapes skin off from another spot on the body and puts it on the damaged area.

Try This! You can do a similar experiment with two apples. Holding one apple, make a small cut in one area and peel a bit of skin off another part of the same apple. Leave the other apple uncut and with the skin on. Put them both in a safe place and watch them over the next few days. The first apple will start to decompose around the areas without skin. The skin of the uncut apple is protecting the apple from injury.

BURPING BAGS

DIFFICULTY LEVEL: MEDIUM
TIME: 10 MINUTES

MATERIALS

- Large resealable bag
- ½ cup white vinegar
- Food coloring (optional)
- 2 teaspoons baking soda
- Paper towel or coffee filter

 Have you ever burped at the wrong moment, like when you were in a movie theater or at dinner? A burp is the release of gas that has built up in your stomach. The gas needs to escape, so you let it out in a big BURP. In this activity, you are going to make a fake burp in a bag!

 Caution: This activity might get messy! Consider doing it outside or in a room that is easy to clean up.

STEPS

1. Pour the vinegar into the bag. Add a few drops of food coloring if you are using it to more easily see what happens in the bag.

2. Place the paper towel or coffee filter on a flat surface. Then place the baking soda in the center of the towel or filter. Carefully grab the corners and pick it up. Fold over the corners to close it. You now have a packet containing the baking soda.

3. Place your baking soda packet in the bag.

4. Seal the bag firmly and wait for it to burp! The bag will puff up as it fills with air before letting out a belch.

HOWS & WHYS: Baking soda reacts with vinegar to produce a gas called carbon dioxide. That is the same gas you breathe out when you exhale or burp. When there is enough carbon dioxide in the bag, it will escape through the seal and make a burping sound.

STEAM CONNECTION: You are creating a chemical reaction by mixing two chemicals to create a different chemical. Vinegar is an acid and baking soda is an alkali. Acids react with alkalies. Scientists use the pH scale to measure how acidic or alkaline something is. Acids have a lower pH value and alkalies have a higher pH value.

Try This! What happens if you try the same experiment in a glass jar with a tight lid instead of the resealable bag? Does the gas escape in a burp?

BIG BLUE EGG

DIFFICULTY LEVEL: MEDIUM
TIME: 15 MINUTES
(PLUS 2 DAYS OF
PREPARATION AND 1 DAY
OF OBSERVATION)

MATERIALS

- 1 raw egg in the shell
- 1 cup white vinegar
- Large spoon
- Large glass jar with lid
- Water
- Blue food coloring
- Paper towel

? Water is important for many parts of your body. The heart pumps blood around the body to deliver oxygen and water. Another way that water travels around the body is through **OSMOSIS**. Let's observe the process of osmosis by changing the color and size of an egg.

STEPS

1. Remove the shell from the raw egg by soaking the egg in the vinegar for 24 to 48 hours. Once the shell is completely gone, remove the egg from the vinegar with a large spoon. Gently place the egg in the jar.

2. Add enough water to the jar to cover the egg. Then add a few drops of food coloring to turn the water bright blue. Put the lid on the jar and set the jar aside.

3. Leave the egg in this mixture for about 24 hours so it has time to soak in the water and gain color.

4. After 24 hours, use the large spoon to remove your egg from the blue mixture. The egg should be bigger and a different color. If you dry it with a paper towel you will see that it doesn't leak. If you like, you can pop the egg. You will see that the yolk is still yellow, but the white and outer membrane are completely blue!

HOWS & WHYS: Osmosis is the movement of water through a semi-permeable membrane. A membrane is a film of tissue. **CELL MEMBRANES** separate the inside of a cell from the outside of a cell. "Semi-permeable" membranes let some things, like water, pass through them. Semi-permeable membranes are like window screens, which allow air and light to come in, but keep bugs and leaves out. An impermeable membrane won't allow any movement of water across it. In this activity, the yolk is impermeable, whereas the white and outer membrane are semi-permeable.

STEAM CONNECTION: Your kidneys use osmosis to filter your blood to keep it clean. Human bodies aren't the only bodies that use osmosis! Most plants and animals use osmosis to move important fluids and nutrients around in their bodies.

Try This! There are other ways to watch osmosis in action! Leave raisins in a bowl of water overnight. What happens to them?

HOMEMADE VOCAL CORDS

DIFFICULTY LEVEL: MEDIUM
TIME: 10 MINUTES

MATERIALS

- Plastic or paper cups
- Rubber bands in different sizes
- Packing tape or craft tape

 People play beautiful music on guitars by plucking the strings. When the strings are plucked, they vibrate and make noise. The vocal cords in your neck work in much the same way. When you speak, the cords vibrate to create the sound of your voice. In this activity you will create your very own "vocal cords" to play with.

STEPS

1. Make the first vocal cord by wrapping a rubber band around the cup from top to bottom. It should pass over the mouth of the cup and under the bottom of the cup. If the band is loose, secure it to the cup with tape. Pluck the rubber band where it stretches across the mouth of the cup. Notice what it sounds like.

2. Now make another vocal cord by using a new cup and a different-sized rubber band. You can use your cups and elastic bands to make as many cords as you like.

3. Experiment with the different sounds that the different bands make when you pluck them. Which bands make the higher sounds—the thin ones or the thick ones?

HOWS & WHYS: When you talk, you breathe out. This air passes over the vocal cords and makes them vibrate, making a sound. In the activity, you may have noticed that a wider rubber band makes a deeper sound. As you get older, your vocal cords get longer and fatter, so your voice sounds deeper.

AWESOME HUMAN BODY SCIENCE EXPERIMENTS FOR KIDS

STEAM CONNECTION: Many musical instruments use strings to create sounds. Musicians use different methods to make the strings move, such as plucking or strumming. Did you know the piano has strings in it? Each key is connected to a string of a different length.

Try This! Try talking while you are breathing in, instead of while you are letting your breath out. It isn't very easy, is it? Now try whispering. When you whisper you aren't using your vocal cords at all.

FILL YOUR LUNGS

DIFFICULTY LEVEL: MEDIUM
TIME: 30 MINUTES

MATERIALS

- 2-liter bottle, empty
- Water
- Permanent marker
- Length of rubber tubing, at least 2 feet long
- Measuring jug
- Large container, like the bath or kitchen sink

 When you take a deep breath, you can feel your chest stretching. Your chest makes itself bigger to fit the air you are breathing in. In this activity, you will explore your **LUNG CAPACITY**—the maximum amount of air you take into your lungs at one time.

STEPS

1. First, prepare your bottle. Pour about ¾ cup (approximately 6 fluid ounces) of water into the bottle. With your marker, draw a line at the top of the water, then label it "6 ounces."

2. Add another ¾ cup of water to the bottle. Draw another line at the top of the water. Label that line "12 ounces."

3. Repeat this process of adding ¾ cup of water and marking the water level until you completely fill the bottle.

4. Fill up your bath or sink with water.

5. Cover the top of the bottle with your hand so no water can escape. Then turn the bottle upside down and put it in the bath or sink. Don't remove your hand from the opening until it is completely underwater. When you pull your hand out, there shouldn't be any air in the bottle.

6. Without taking the bottle out of the water, insert the rubber tube into the bottle opening. Hold one end of the tube in your hand while you put the other end into the bottle. Make sure no water gets into the tube.

7. Now take a deep breath and blow as hard as you can into the tube. Blow until you don't have any air in your lungs.

8. There is now air in the bottle. The lines will tell you how much. Did you blow out the equivalent of 6 ounces of air? Or more?

HOWS & WHYS: Your lung capacity is the amount of air you can breathe in and out of your lungs. Lung capacity affects how quickly you get oxygen to your body. Athletes train regularly to increase their lung capacity, which makes it easier for them to breathe when they are competing in races or games.

STEAM CONNECTION: When people want to go deep under the sea, they use special cylinders of air called scuba tanks to help them breathe. As they go deeper and deeper, there's more pressure on them from the sea above. This pressure affects the air in the tanks and how the gases are absorbed in their bodies. They must be careful not to injure themselves by swimming back to the surface too quickly.

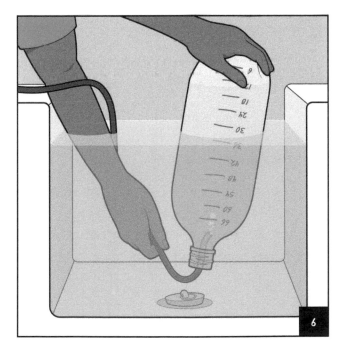

Try This! Try doing five super-deep breaths every day for a week, then repeat the lung capacity experiment. Has your lung capacity increased in any noticeable way? Does the water level go down more, or is it the same as before?

MIX IT UP!

MATERIALS

- Mixing bowl
- 2 tablespoons white flour
- 2 tablespoons warm water
- Spoon
- 2 jars or cups
- Iodine antiseptic solution
- Eyedropper
- Test tube or other narrow container, like a small jar or small plate
- Plate

 In "Taste Test" on page 38, you discovered how saliva affects the taste of food. That is not saliva's only job. In this experiment, you'll discover how saliva helps break down food.

STEPS

1. In the bowl, mix the flour and warm water to make your flour mixture.

2. Spoon 1 teaspoon of your flour mixture into your test tube or jar. Use the eyedropper to add 1 or 2 drops of iodine solution to the mixture. Shake or mix the liquid until it turns blue.

3. Now gather as much saliva in your mouth as you can. Carefully spit it onto the plate.

4. Place another teaspoon of your flour mixture into the saliva (not the blue stuff). Mix well to combine the saliva and the flour mixture.

5. Add 1 or 2 drops of iodine to the saliva mixture. Does it turn blue? Is it as dark as the first one?

6. Every half hour, add 1 or 2 drops of iodine to the saliva mixture. How long does it take to stop turning blue? You should notice a slight decrease in color every time you do it. How much time does it take for the flour not to change color at all?

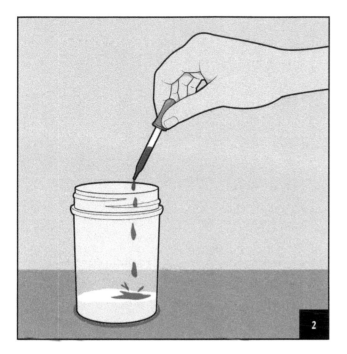

STEAM CONNECTION: You used the iodine solution to turn your saliva mixture blue. Iodine is also used in first aid as an antiseptic. It is often applied to skin or tissue to help prevent infection.

Try This! Take a bite of bread and rank the sweetness of it on a scale of from 1 to 10. Now chew it slowly. Keep the bread in your mouth without swallowing it. Can you chew 20 times? How does the bread taste now? It should start to taste sweeter because your saliva breaks down the starch into glucose. Your mouth tastes the glucose as sweet.

CENTERED EYES

DIFFICULTY LEVEL: MEDIUM
TIME: 10 MINUTES

MATERIALS

- A partner
- Beanbag or soft ball
- 2 eye patches or blindfolds

 Our eyes are amazing! They let us see all kinds of things. For example, we can see different colors and lines. We can also see depth, which means we can tell if something is far away or near. In this activity, you're going to learn how having two eyes helps you see depth.

STEPS

1. Stand a few feet away from your partner. Start by throwing the beanbag or ball back and forth to each other.

2. Next, cover one of your eyes with an eye patch or blindfold. Have your partner do the same.

3. Throw the ball or beanbag to each other. What happens now that you both have covered an eye? Is it more difficult to catch?

HOWS & WHYS: Your brain usually receives information from both eyes and the combined effect is called **BINOCULAR VISION**. Seeing with both eyes helps you understand how far away objects are. When you cover one eye, your brain doesn't get as much information. Using only one eye makes it more difficult to understand how far away the object is.

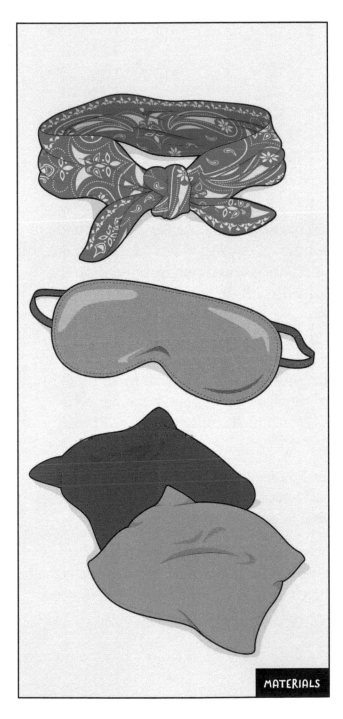

MATERIALS

Try This! Hold a finger out at arm's length. Line it up with an object in the distance, such as a tree or a streetlight pole. Now close one eye. What happens to your finger and the object? Do they move out of line? Try this experiment again with the other eye.

HARD HEAD

DIFFICULTY LEVEL: MEDIUM
TIME: 20 MINUTES

MATERIALS

- ➔ 1 seedless watermelon
- ➔ Old helmet that you don't want anymore, like a bike or hockey helmet

 Our skulls protect our brains. If we didn't have a skull, our brain would be damaged by the slightest bonk on the head. The brain controls our body's functions, so our skulls do a very important job! Let's use a watermelon to see how we can help keep our brains safe.

 Caution: This activity is messy. Do it outside or in an area that is easy to clean up. Do not eat the watermelon once you have dropped it on the ground or a dirty floor.

STEPS

1. Begin by testing the strength of the hard watermelon skin. Tap your knuckles on the skin. What happens? Does it break? Now punch it. What happens? Does it break?

2. Next, place the helmet on the watermelon and fasten it tightly. Drop the watermelon onto the ground with the helmet on. What happened? Did it break?

3. If the watermelon did not break, remove the helmet. Now throw the watermelon to the ground again. Notice the difference when it does not have a helmet to protect it.

HOWS & WHYS: Like the inside of a watermelon, our brains are soft. The brain is mostly water and fat. It is surrounded by a swimming pool of special liquid called cerebrospinal fluid. This fluid stops the brain from bumping against the hard skull.

STEAM CONNECTION: There are different types of helmets to keep our heads and brains safe. Some are simple helmets made of hard foam, while others are complex helmets that use special technology. Many ski helmets use a special technology called MIPS, which stands for Multi-Directional Impact Protection System.

Try This! Can you find two pieces of pink watermelon flesh that are the same size? Put each of them in a jar. Fill one jar with water and leave the other without water. Put the lids on and shake the jars. How do the pieces of watermelon look now? Does one look less damaged than the other?

MOVING MUSCLES

DIFFICULTY LEVEL: MEDIUM
TIME: 15 MINUTES

MATERIALS

- 3 long cardboard tubes, like paper towel tubes or wrapping paper tubes
- 2 long balloons, like for making balloon animals
- 1 long piece of string, at least 4 feet
- Scissors
- 1 glove (any type of glove is fine)
- Permanent marker

 Our muscles are connected to bones all over the body. We know that muscles help us move, but how? In this activity, you'll make a model arm that shows you how it works.

Caution: Sharp scissors should be handled only with adult supervision.

STEPS

1. For this model, the cardboard tubes will be your bones. You have three bones in your arm: ulna, radius, and humerus. Use the marker to label each tube with a name of one of the arm bones.

2. Using the scissors, carefully poke a hole into one end of each tube.

3. Place your tubes in a row, with the humerus in the middle. Thread the string through the holes to join the three tubes. You're making an elbow.

4. The radius and ulna are your forearm. They make up the arm between your wrist and elbow. The humerus is the upper arm, between your elbow and shoulder. Arrange the tubes so they look like an arm, with the humerus in one direction and the radius and ulna in the other direction.

5. Blow the balloons one-third of the way, then tie them closed. Push the air to the middle to create empty space on either side.

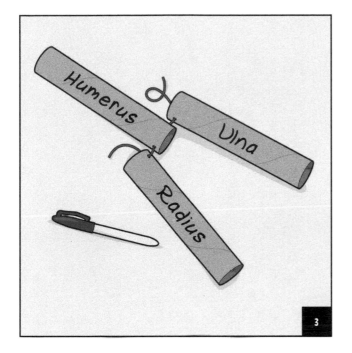

6. Attach each end of a balloon to the underside of the humerus to represent your tricep muscle. Label it with the marker.

7. Tie the other balloon to the top of the humerus, which is at the far end from the ulna and radius, to represent your bicep. Label it with the marker.

8. Put the glove on the end of the radius and ulna.

9. Now, move your model arm to open and close it. What happens to the balloons when you bend the elbow? What happens to the balloons when you straighten the elbow?

HOWS & WHYS: Your muscles contract to move your bones. When you open the arm model, you can see that the bicep stretches and the tricep gets shorter. Your tricep muscle is creating the movement. When you bend your arm model, the bicep gets shorter and the tricep gets longer. This time, the bicep is contracting to create the movement.

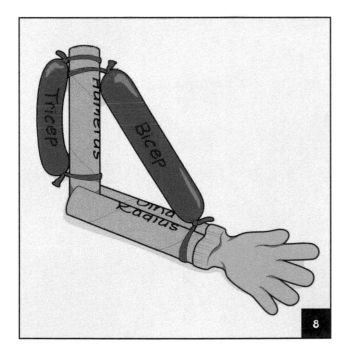

CONTINUED

STEAM CONNECTION: All types of muscle tissue have proteins called actin and myosin. The actin and myosin are like two strings. They work together to make the muscle contractions.

Try This! You can use these same instructions to make a model leg. The tricep balloon will represent the quadriceps muscle on the top of your thigh. Instead of the humerus in the arm, the single bone in the leg is called the femur. Label the two other bones "tibia" and "fibula."

BUILDING BLOCKS

DIFFICULTY LEVEL: MEDIUM
TIME: 15 MINUTES

MATERIALS

- Toy construction bricks, like Legos or MEGA Bloks, in a variety of colors

 Chemical elements join to form compound molecules. One example is how hydrogen and oxygen join to form water. In this activity, you're going to use toy bricks to represent chemical elements that are found in your body. Let's make some compound molecules!

STEPS

1. Sort your bricks by color. You'll need blue for nitrogen, white for oxygen, red for carbon, and green for hydrogen.

2. Make a model of a nitrogen molecule by joining 2 blue bricks together.

3. Next, create a model of an oxygen molecule by joining 2 white bricks together.

4. Now make a carbon dioxide model. A carbon dioxide molecule includes two oxygen molecules and one carbon, so you'll need 2 white bricks and 1 red one brick. The red brick goes in the middle.

5. Finally, make a water model. Every molecule of water has two hydrogen molecules and one oxygen molecule. Join 2 green bricks and 1 white brick together. The white brick goes in the middle.

HOWS & WHYS: The main chemical elements that make up our body are hydrogen, carbon, oxygen, and nitrogen. They can combine in different ways to make different things. For example, glucose molecules have carbon, hydrogen, and oxygen atoms in them. When we eat glucose in our food and use it as fuel, our body breaks that glucose down into carbon dioxide and water.

STEAM CONNECTION: CHEMISTRY studies the way different substances, or chemicals, interact. Chemists use chemical formulas to show what elements combine to make compound molecules. For example, nitrogen gas is two nitrogen atoms joined together. The chemical formula for nitrogen is N_2. Carbon dioxide gas is one carbon atom and two oxygen atoms joined together. The chemical formula for carbon dioxide is CO_2.

Try This! Use your blocks to make models of different compound molecules. Can you make a super-complicated molecule like a protein? Or a carbohydrate molecule such as glucose? Ask an adult to help you look up these molecules on the internet.

THUMBS UP!

DIFFICULTY LEVEL: MEDIUM
TIME: 15 MINUTES

MATERIALS

→ You!

Do you know how amazing your hands are? There are so many things they can do, including very delicate tasks like writing or painting! One motion that our hands make is called opposition. Opposition is when we touch our fingers to our thumbs. In this activity, you will discover the power of such a simple motion.

STEPS

1. Touch your thumb to your little finger. This position is called opposition.

2. Touch your thumb to each of your fingers, one at a time.

3. Now pretend your thumb can't touch the other fingers. It can only stay by the side of your hand. It can't move across and connect with your fingers. Then, try completing some everyday activities, like opening a door, writing, getting dressed, or eating. How do these activities feel when you can't use your thumb?

HOWS & WHYS: Humans have **OPPOSABLE THUMBS**, which means we can use opposition with our hands. As you noticed in this activity, we use opposition for many things. In fact, it's one of the reasons we're the dominant species on the planet. This special motion allows us to grasp things easily. It allows us to create and use tools that other animals can't.

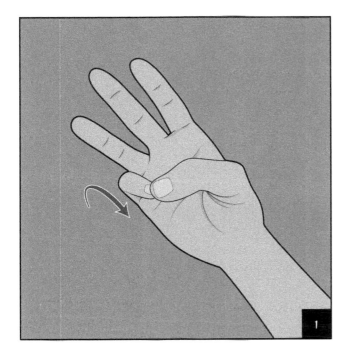

Try This! Hold your hands in front of you with the palms facing down. Now turn them over so the palms face upwards. This position is called supination. Turn your palms facedown again. This position is called pronation. Try doing some everyday motions without using this motion of supination or pronation.

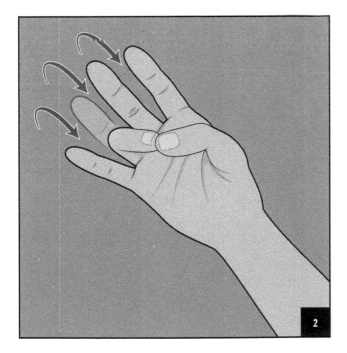

LUNG FUN

DIFFICULTY LEVEL:
CHALLENGING
TIME: 30 MINUTES

MATERIALS

- 1 big balloon (12 inches)
- Scissors
- 2-liter bottle, empty
- Masking tape
- 2 straws
- 2 small balloons (9 inches)
- Rubber bands
- Modeling clay

 The respiratory system moves air in and out of your body. Let's make a model of the lungs to see how you inhale (breathe in) and exhale (breathe out).

 Caution: Sharp scissors should be handled only under adult supervision.

STEPS

1. Tie a knot in the end of the big balloon while it is uninflated. Cut off the end of the balloon and discard it. Keep the piece of balloon with the knot tied in the neck.

2. Carefully cut off the bottom of the bottle so that it is open on the wide end with the lid still attached. Discard the bottom of the bottle.

3. Stretch the cut balloon over the bottle opening. The knot should be in the center. Secure the balloon to the bottle with the masking tape, making sure there are no holes to let air in.

4. Insert a straw into the opening of one of the small balloons. Use a rubber band to hold it in place. Repeat this activity with the other straw and the other small balloon.

5. Remove the lid from the bottle. Ask an adult to make two holes in the lid. Each hole should each be big enough to fit one straw.

6. Push a straw through each hole so that the balloons will be inside the bottle when you put the lid back on. Then, use another rubber band to secure the straws in place.

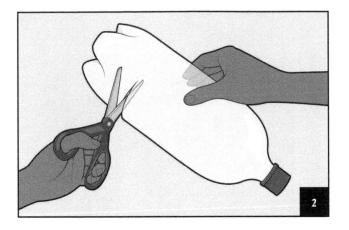

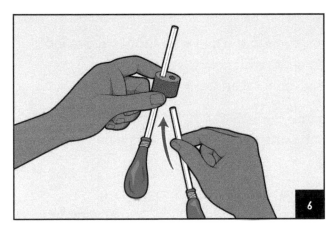

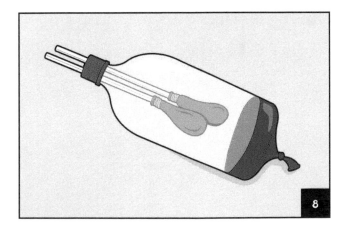

7. Make sure no air can get in through the sides of the holes. If there are any gaps, fill them with the modeling clay.

8. Place the lid on the bottle. The balloons should be hanging inside the bottle.

9. You have built a working model of your lungs! Pull the knot of the big balloon. What happens?

HOWS & WHYS: In this model, the small balloons are your lungs and the big balloon is your diaphragm. The diaphragm is a muscle that sits below your lungs. As you pull the big balloon, you're recreating the action of "breathing in." It shows how the diaphragm opens up your lungs.

STEAM CONNECTION: Scientists often make models of things they're trying to understand. The model can help them see things they can't observe directly, such as **very big things like galaxies or very small things like molecules.**

Try This! Clog the straws with some modeling clay. What happens when you move the diaphragm?

THE JOY OF JOINTS

DIFFICULTY LEVEL:
CHALLENGING
TIME: 20 MINUTES

MATERIALS

- Chopstick
- Sponge ball
- Tape
- Plastic cup or small bowl

 A joint is a part of the body that connects bones. Joints allow you to bend your limbs and other body parts. There are six types of joints in your body, which create different motions like twisting and bending. Your hip is a ball-and-socket joint that connects your leg to your body. This type of joint allows a lot of movement. Check out how it works!

STEPS

1. Attach the chopstick to the ball with tape to represent your upper leg bone, which is called the femur. The femur has a ball-shaped end.

2. Place the ball into the cup or bowl to represent the socket. Your hip bone has a socket that the ball of your femur sits in.

3. How many ways can you move the chopstick? Try moving it back and forth, side to side, and around in a circle. See if you can copy these movements with your own legs. Can you do all of them? Are some harder than others?

HOWS & WHYS: Joints make it possible for your bones to change their positions. Joints are made of flexible materials like cartilage, ligaments, and tendons.

STEAM CONNECTION: By creating a working model, you are using engineering to explore how joints work. Joints aren't only found in the body. You can find them all around us, like to open and close doors and to attach wheels to a wagon.

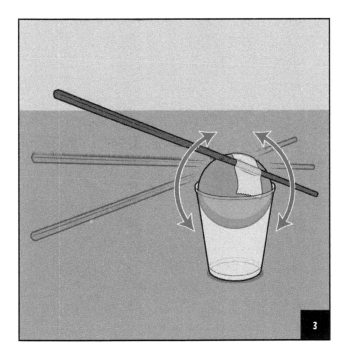

Try This! A hinge joint makes opening and closing movements, like the hinges on doors. Your knees and elbows are hinge joints. Make a model of a hinge joint by folding a piece of cardboard in half. You can open it and close it along that fold, just like you can bend your elbow. Hinge joints are very sturdy but only move in one direction.

DNA DETECTOR

MATERIALS

- 2 fresh strawberries
- Resealable plastic bag
- Liquid dish soap
- Water
- Salt
- Coffee filter
- Plastic cup
- Cold rubbing alcohol (keep it in the freezer until you're ready to use it)
- Spoon

 Cells are small units of living material that do important jobs in our bodies. But how do cells know what to do? Cells come with their own set of instructions, called DNA (deoxyribonucleic acid). The DNA tells the cells what to do. For example, your DNA tells your hair cells which color hair to be and tells your eye cells which color eyes you have. In this activity, you're going to extract DNA, just like a scientist in a laboratory.

 Caution: Do not drink the rubbing alcohol! Ask an adult to help you with the alcohol.

STEPS

1. Trim or slice off any green or unripe parts of the strawberries. Remove any parts that look brown and mushy. You should be left with only the red fruit.

2. Put the strawberries in the bag. Seal it tight.

3. Ready for the fun part? Squash the strawberries in the bag. Don't overdo it and squirt them all over the place. Make sure to squash them into a uniform pulp. This activity should take about 2 minutes.

4. Mix 2 teaspoons of the liquid dish soap with ½ cup of water and 1 teaspoon of salt.

5. Add 2 teaspoons of the dish soap mixture to your strawberry pulp to finish breaking up the cells that you began breaking when you smashed the strawberries.

6. Reseal the bag and do some more strawberry smashing. Try to avoid making soap bubbles.

7. Place your coffee filter in the plastic cup.

8. Pour your strawberry pulp into the coffee filter so that it drips into the cup. You can twist the top of the filter and push it downwards to squeeze the liquid out.

9. Slowly pour the rubbing alcohol into the cup. You should pour an equal amount of alcohol as there is strawberry pulp. Do not stir or shake the cup.

10. After a few seconds, you should see a whitish substance forming on top of the liquid. This substance is the DNA you have extracted! Use your spoon to scoop it out.

CONTINUED

HOWS & WHYS: You used the dish soap to lyse the cell, which means you broke down the outer membrane. Then, the alcohol separated the DNA from the rest of the strawberry cells. The DNA precipitated out of the mixture, which means it became solid. Now you can see the DNA!

STEAM CONNECTION: DNA lives in little packets called chromosomes. Humans have 23 pairs of chromosomes, which comes to 46 in total. For a long time, scientists knew about DNA, but they didn't know very many details about it. Now scientists know a lot more about what the chromosomes do, like which ones are responsible for your eye color.

Try This! Can you remove the DNA from other fruit? Try this activity with a banana and see what happens.

MAKE A MODEL SPINE

DIFFICULTY LEVEL:
CHALLENGING
TIME: 30 MINUTES

MATERIALS

- ➜ A few pieces of paper
- ➜ Scissors
- ➜ Cardboard egg cartons (24 cups) or a pool noodle
- ➜ Long piece of string, at least 2 feet long

 Your back moves in many ways. It can move from side to side, backward and forward, and even do wriggly movements. Your neck allows you to move your head in lots of directions, too. In "The Joy of Joints" on page 84, you saw how a few different joints in the body work. Now it's time to explore how the joints in your back and neck create so many amazing movements.

 Caution: Sharp scissors should be handled only under adult supervision.

STEPS

1. Cut out 10 circles of paper. Each circle should be 1 to 2 inches in diameter.

2. Poke a small hole in the center of each circle. Set the circles aside.

3. If you're using egg cartons, cut each cup out to create individual cups. Poke a hole on one side of each cup and another hole on the opposite side. If you're using a pool noodle, cut it into 24 pieces that are each 1 inch long.

4. Thread the string through one egg cup. The string should pass through both holes in the cup.

5. Next, thread the string through the hole in one of the paper circles.

6. Repeat steps 4 and 5 until you have threaded all the egg cups or pool noodle pieces together with the paper circles.

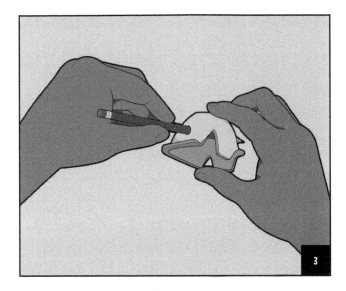

7. Tie a knot on each end of the string.

8. Now you can play with your model spine. How many different ways can you move it? Can you make those movements in real life?

> **HOWS & WHYS:** The egg cups represent the bones in your spine, called vertebrae. The string of bones (or egg cups) can move in lots of different ways, just like your back. The pieces of paper represent intervertebral discs, protective pads between the vertebrae.

> **STEAM CONNECTION:** Your spinal cord is a bundle of nerves that runs from your brain down your spine. The spinal cord sends and receives messages from all over your body.

Try This! Your spine is divided into sections. Your neck has 7 cervical vertebrae. Color the first 7 egg cups orange. Below your neck you have 12 thoracic vertebrae. They're connected to your ribs. Color them purple. Below that you have 5 lumbar vertebrae. Color them yellow. Now you can see the different sections of spine on your model.

MAKE A MODEL HEART

DIFFICULTY LEVEL:
CHALLENGING
TIME: 30 MINUTES

MATERIALS

- A helper or two (you might need some extra hands!)
- 2 plastic bottles, each 2 liters
- Scissors
- Balloons
- Packing tape
- 2 rigid straws, like metal drinking straws
- 2 small plastic bags
- Red- and blue-colored liquid, like liquid paint or food coloring in water
- Permanent marker
- Large container, like a bathtub or the kitchen sink

 Did you know your heart has four sections called chambers? In this experiment, you're going to see how the four chambers are connected. You're also going to make a valve. A valve allows liquid to travel one way, but not the other way. We have valves in our hearts that stop blood from going the wrong way.

 Caution: Sharp scissors should only be handled under adult supervision. This activity is messy. Do it outside or in an area that is easy to clean up.

STEPS

1. Cut both bottles in half, then take the lids off the top halves. Discard the bottom halves of the bottles.

2. Cut the top off 2 balloons. Discard the top parts that have the balloon neck. You should end up with 2 pieces of balloon.

3. Put a balloon over the neck of each plastic bottle half. Secure the balloons to the bottles with tape. Make sure the seal around the edge of the balloon and the bottle neck is watertight.

4. Poke a small hole in the middle of each balloon piece.

5. Turn the bottles upside down so the balloon is underneath and the opening is at the top. Set the bottles aside.

6. Next, insert 1 straw into each plastic bag. The bottom of the straw should be halfway down the bag.

7. Tape the bags with the straw in them around each bottle neck to create a pouch under the bottle neck. Make sure the straw is sticking out of the side of the bottle and it's sealed watertight. (The water is going to go into the bottle opening, through the hole in the balloon, into the bag, then out of the straw.)

8. Now you have 2 bottle tops with plastic bags underneath them. Tape the bottles together. There should be a straw sticking out of each bag.

9. Now label your chambers. The 2 bottles are the left atrium and the right atrium. You can write "LA" and "RA" on them. The bags are the left ventricle and the right ventricle. Write "LV" and "RV" on them. Make sure you have the LA and LV on one side, and the RA and RV on the other.

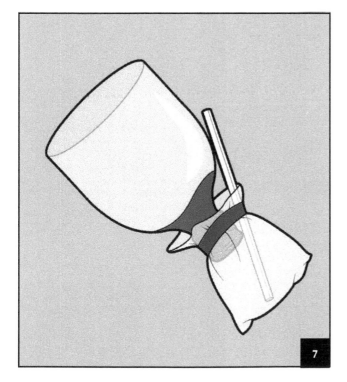

CONTINUED

10. Complete this next step over the sink or outside. Pour the red liquid into the bottle marked RA. Pour the blue liquid in the bottle marked LA.

11. Watch the water drain through your balloon valves and into the bags. Notice if you see any water leaking out anywhere and repair any leaks with tape.

12. When both bags are full, squeeze them gently at the same time. You might need a spare pair of hands to help you. What happens?

HOWS & WHYS: This model represents your heart. Your blood (the red liquid) flows into your right atrium through a valve into your right ventricle. The blood then travels to your lungs, where oxygen comes in and carbon dioxide goes out. Then, the blood (the blue liquid) returns to your heart so it can be pumped around your body. The blood flows into the left atrium, through another valve and into your left ventricle. When you squeeze the bags, the liquid should flow out of the straws, which represent the big arteries in your body.

STEAM CONNECTION: Doctors use special technology called heart bypass machines when they perform surgery on people's hearts. These machines pump the blood around the body while the surgeons operate on the heart.

Try This! Connect the two atriums with a long, bendy straw. Insert either end of the straw into the opening of each bottle and make sure no water escapes. This model represents how babies get oxygen before they are born. They don't use lungs but instead get their oxygen from the mother's body.

PRINGLE PINHOLE

MATERIALS

- Chip can, like a Pringles can or similar tube
- Thumb tack
- Translucent paper, such as wax paper or parchment paper
- Scissors
- Sticky tape
- Paper towels
- Aluminum foil

 Your eyes concentrate light into one spot, then send the information to your brain though your optic nerve. In this activity, you will learn how this transfer works.

Caution: Ask an adult to help you with the sharp thumb tack and scissors. These items should be handled only under adult supervision.

STEPS

1. Remove the lid from the chip can and clean out the can. Remove any crumbs and wipe the inside clean with a towel.

2. Use the thumb tack to poke a hole in the bottom of the can. Center the hole as best you can.

3. Cut the bottom off the can, approximately 2 inches from the base. You now have one short tube with the base, and a longer tube with open ends.

4. Cover the open end of the short piece with the translucent paper.

5. Now stick the short tube back onto the long tube. It should be exactly where it was before, except now there's a piece of translucent paper in between the tubes.

6. Cover the tube in aluminum foil, except for the hole at the end, so that no light can get through.

AWESOME HUMAN BODY SCIENCE EXPERIMENTS FOR KIDS

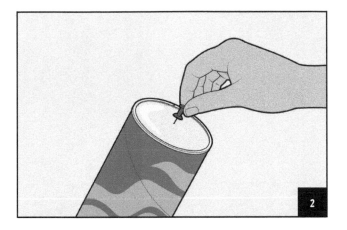

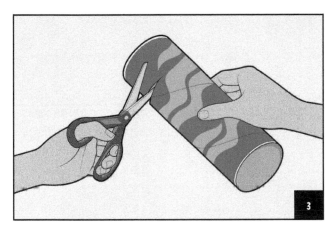

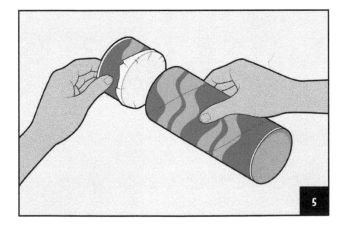

7. Hold the pinhole up to one eye and close your other eye so that you are using the tube like a telescope. You should be able to see things on the translucent paper, but everything should be upside down.

HOWS & WHYS: The pupil in our eye works like the hole in the chip can. When the image goes through the pupil, it's turned upside down. The image information travels to the brain through the optic nerve. The brain turns the image the right way up.

STEAM CONNECTION: Pinhole cameras like your chip can are used during solar eclipses. They cast a shadow on the ground with a small dot of light in the middle. When the moon passes the sun, a shadow will pass over the dot on the ground, allowing you to see an eclipse without staring at the sun.

Try This! Make a pinhole camera with a dark piece of cardboard. Place a lamp on one end of a table and the cardboard on the other end. Put a clear glass bowl between the lamp and the cardboard. Darken the room and turn the lamp on. You'll see an upside-down image of the lamp on the cardboard!

MAKE A NEURON

DIFFICULTY LEVEL:
CHALLENGING
TIME: 20 MINUTES

MATERIALS

- 1 long pipe cleaner, about 8 inches long
- 2 medium-length pipe cleaners, about 4 inches long
- 10 or 12 small pipe cleaners (2 different colors), about 2 inches long
- 5 or 6 very small pipe cleaners, about 1 inch long

 Neurons are a message system that connects your brain to the rest of your body. The neurons send signals and receive signals. In this activity, you're going to make a model to see all the different parts of a neuron.

STEPS

1. Roll one of the medium pipe cleaners into a ball to represent the cell body of the neuron.

2. Stick the long pipe cleaner through the ball so that the ball is in the center of the long pipe cleaner.

3. Bring the two ends of the long pipe cleaner together and twist them to connect them. This connection is the axon of the neuron.

4. Poke the small pipe cleaners through the ball of medium pipe cleaner. The ball should be in the middle of each of the short pipe cleaners. These extensions are the dendrites of the neuron. They might look like little fingers or arms.

5. Twist the very small pipe cleaners around the big pipe cleaner to make rings around it. These rings are myelin sheaths.

6. Make another spiky ball like you did with the dendrites. This other ball goes at the other end of the long pipe cleaner. This other ball is the signal end. Each pipe cleaner has a synaptic terminal at the end.

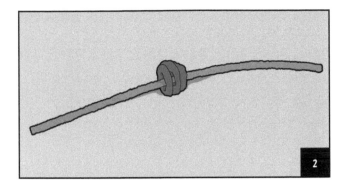

HOWS & WHYS: The cell body is like a control center for the neuron. Messages travel up and down the axons as electrical pulses. At the end of each axon is a synaptic terminal, which transmits the messages to another neuron. The dendrites receive inputs and fire a signal to your brain. The myelin sheath is a layer that sits around the neuron, helping messages travel quickly.

STEAM CONNECTION: Some computers are modeled on the human brain. They use artificial neural networks to learn by themselves.

Try This! Make another neuron and see if you can fit it together with the neuron you already made. The synaptic terminal of one neuron sends a message across a gap to the dendrites of another neuron.

MAKE A STETHOSCOPE

DIFFICULTY LEVEL:
CHALLENGING
TIME: 20 MINUTES

MATERIALS

- Small funnel with a 1-inch opening, such as a kitchen funnel
- Piece of wax paper or other thin paper
- Rubber band
- Cardboard toilet paper roll
- Packing tape
- A partner

 A stethoscope is a tool that health-care providers use to listen to the inside of people's bodies. What do they hear inside your body? You're about to find out! Be sure to ask for permission before you use your homemade stethoscope on someone else's body.

STEPS

1. Wrap the big end of the funnel in the paper and secure it with the rubber band.

2. Place the cardboard roll over the small end of the funnel and secure it with tape.

3. Put the big end of the funnel on the left side of your partner's chest. Bring your ear to the small end. Do you hear anything?

4. Try putting it on the other side of your partner's chest. Ask them to breathe in and out. What do you hear?

HOWS & WHYS: A stethoscope makes small sounds louder. When you used your stethoscope, you could hear the heart valves opening and closing. You also heard the air going in and out of the lungs. The amplified sounds travel through the stethoscope to your ears.

STEAM CONNECTION: An obstetrician is a doctor who cares for pregnant people. When someone is pregnant, an obstetrician places a stethoscope on their belly to hear the baby's heartbeat.

Try This! Take the paper off the funnel of your stethoscope. Does it make any difference? The paper is called a diaphragm. It makes it easier to hear sounds that are high pitched. In a real stethoscope, the diaphragm is not made of paper.

FILTER FRENZY

DIFFICULTY LEVEL:
CHALLENGING
TIME: 30 MINUTES

MATERIALS

- 3 cups or bowls
- Woolen scarf
- Soil or dirt mixed with water to create a muddy liquid
- Notebook
- Pencil
- Piece of cotton material, like a cotton T-shirt
- Coffee filter

 Your kidneys are a pair of bean-shaped organs. They are located below your ribs and behind your belly. As your blood passes through the kidneys, they filter out waste and control the amount of water in your blood. In this activity, you will experiment with filters to see how kidneys work.

 Caution: Check that the scarf you are going to use is washable. If not, it will be ruined. This activity might get messy. Consider doing it outside or in an area that can be easily cleaned.

STEPS

1. Cover the top of one of the cups or bowls with the scarf. Pour some of the muddy water onto the scarf so that it drips into the bowl underneath. How much of it goes though? Does some of the mud stay caught in the scarf? How clean is the water in the bowl? Record your observations in your notebook.

2. Next, extend the cotton over a cup or bowl. Pour some muddy water on the cotton so it drips into the bowl. How much mud does it catch? And how clean is the water in the bowl? Is it cleaner than when you used the woolen scarf? Write down your observations.

3. Finally, place the coffee filter over the third cup or bowl. Pour the muddy water into the filter. Once again, observe what happens and note the results.

MATERIALS

HOWS & WHYS: Just like the scarf, the coffee filter, and the cotton, your kidneys filter out waste. Kidneys regulate the amount of water in your blood and direct all the waste of your blood into your bladder. The waste is then removed from your body by peeing it out.

STEAM CONNECTION: People use filters to make sure they have clean water to drink. The town or city where you live uses filtration to help clean your tap water. Some people have an additional filtration system in their homes. If you go camping in the wild, you need a portable filtration system for clean drinking water.

Try This! You've tried different materials as the filter. How about filtering different liquids? What happens when you put things like grass in the liquid? Which is the best material for filtering?

MAKE AN ARTICULATING HAND

DIFFICULTY LEVEL:
CHALLENGING
TIME: 20 MINUTES

MATERIALS

- Cardboard
- Pencil
- 10 to 12 plastic drinking straws
- Spool of string
- Scissors
- Packing tape

 Wiggle your fingers and shake your hands around. How are you making those moves? In this activity, you will build a model to see how your ligaments help you move your fingers.

Caution: Sharp scissors should be used only under adult supervision.

STEPS

1. Using the pencil, trace your hand onto the cardboard. Use scissors to cut along the line you traced. Now you have a cardboard hand.

2. Mark where your joints are on the cardboard hand. Remember, your joints are the places where your bones connect and your fingers bend.

3. Cut pieces of straw to go between the joints in your fingers. Make each piece about 1 inch long. You'll need 3 pieces for each finger and 2 pieces for your thumb. Set the pieces of straw onto the cardboard where you marked your joints.

4. Cut 4 pieces of straw to connect the bases of the cardboard fingers to the wrist. Tape the pieces in place. Cut a shorter piece of straw to connect the base of the thumb to the wrist. Stick this piece in place.

5. Cut a length of string double the length of your hands. Feed the string through one of the straws at the wrist, then through the straws on one finger, then out the other end.

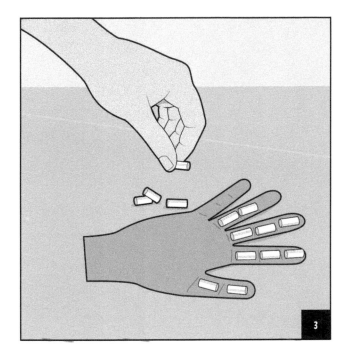

You should have some string sticking out of the straw at the top of the finger. Tie a knot at the end of the string so that the string can't slip back into the straw. Do the same for the other fingers and the thumb.

6. Tape the string to the tips of the fingers and thumb. You should have five strings. Tie them in a knot.

7. Pull the knot of strings and see what happens.

HOWS & WHYS: Ligaments are bands of tough tissue, like the string in your model. Ligaments connect bones to other bones.

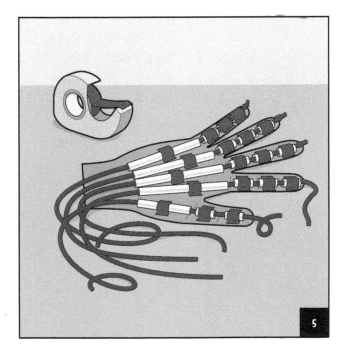

STEAM CONNECTION: Many of your body's joints, including the knees, ankles, elbows, and shoulders, have ligaments around them. Just like a bit of natural engineering, the ligaments help to keep these joints strong and stable.

Try This! Relax your hand and hold it out in front of you. Gently squeeze your arm below your wrist. When you squeeze, you pull on your ligaments, which makes your fingers curl. Try it on a friend. Remember to ask permission and be gentle.

LIGHT BONES

DIFFICULTY LEVEL:
CHALLENGING
TIME: 30 MINUTES
(PLUS 90 MINUTES OF
COOLING TIME)

MATERIALS

- Butter
- Cake pan, about 8 inches wide
- Granulated sugar
- Golden syrup or honey
- Frying pan, nonstick if possible
- Stovetop
- Baking soda
- Wooden spoon

 Bones are hard but light in weight. If they weren't light, our skeletons would be too heavy for us to move. Let's discover just how tough and light our bones are. You're in luck because this activity is super-delicious!

Caution: This experiment involves cooking with heat and requires adult supervision.

STEPS

1. Prepare the cake pan by coating it with 1 teaspoon of butter.

2. Mix 1 cup of the sugar and $\frac{1}{3}$ cup of the golden syrup in the frying pan over low heat. Try not to let the mixture bubble. Mix until all the sugar grains have disappeared.

3. Turn up the heat and simmer until you have an amber-colored caramel.

4. Turn off the heat and add 2 teaspoons of the baking soda. Beat the mixture with a wooden spoon until all the baking soda has disappeared and the mixture is foaming.

5. Immediately scrape the mixture into the prepared cake pan. Be careful because the mixture is very hot.

6. The mixture will continue to bubble. Leave the mixture to cool for 60 to 90 minutes. As it cools, the mixture will harden into a honeycomb.

AWESOME HUMAN BODY SCIENCE EXPERIMENTS FOR KIDS

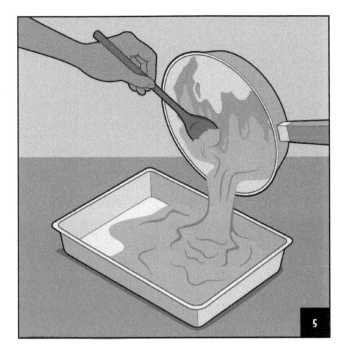

7. Break the honeycomb up so that you can see inside it. This substance is what the center of your bones looks like. After you have done that, you can eat the honeycomb!

HOWS & WHYS: Our bones are light because they have lots of little holes inside them, yet they are still hard because they are made with calcium. The outside of the bones is solid and helps protect the soft inside.

STEAM CONNECTION: Have you ever wondered how birds can fly? If they had heavy bones, they wouldn't be able to get off the ground. Just like us, birds have bones with holes inside. But birds also have hollow legs with bigger air pockets than our bones.

Try This! Put some of the honeycomb in a cardboard tube to represent the hard outside layer of our bones. See how much harder it is to crush or break the honeycomb? The outer part of our bone protects the softer inside.

CLOTTING BLOOD

DIFFICULTY LEVEL:
CHALLENGING
TIME: 30 MINUTES (PLUS
TIME TO ALLOW THE
JELL-O TO SET)

MATERIALS

- 1 packet of red Jell-O mix
- Red paint
- 2 squeeze bottles

 Our blood is made up of different types of cells. This variety in cells helps blood do different jobs. One of those jobs is clotting. Blood clotting is what helps us stop bleeding when we get cut. Let's see how it works.

Caution: Ask an adult to help you make the Jell-O. This activity is messy, so do it outside or on a surface that is easy to clean.

STEPS

1. Prepare the Jell-O according to the directions on the package. Make sure an adult helps you.

2. While the Jell-O is still liquid, pour it into one of the squeeze bottles. Put the nozzle lid back on the bottle, then put the bottle in the fridge. Leave the Jell-O to set for the time mentioned in the directions on the package.

3. Fill the other bottle with paint.

4. Once the Jell-O has set, you're going to squeeze both the bottles either outside or somewhere that is easy to clean, like a kitchen sink.

5. Squeeze both bottles. Which one squirts more easily?

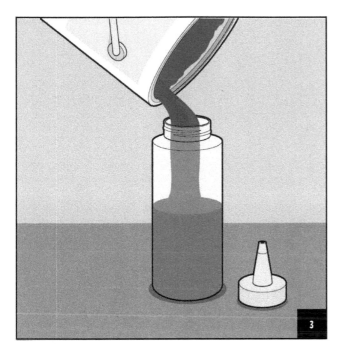

HOWS & WHYS: Inside your body, your blood is liquid. When there is a cut in the skin and blood touches air, blood cells called platelets stick to the edge of the cut. The platelet cells then join to form a plug, or a clot. Clotting is when blood turns solid and stops the flow of liquid. The paint is like liquid blood inside the body. When blood begins to clot, it is more like the Jell-O.

STEAM CONNECTION: In physics, there are three **STATES OF MATTER**: solid, liquid, and gas. Liquids flow and take the shape of their container. When blood is inside the body, it is a liquid. Solids hold their own shape, just like clotted blood.

Try This! Try mixing the liquid paint and the Jell-O and squirting the mixture out of a third bottle. Was it easier or harder to squirt than the plain paint?

Part III

PUTTING IT ALL TOGETHER

You made it to the end of the book! You've done some amazing activities and learned so much along the way. What was your favorite activity? Did you like bending bones or burping bags? You learned that we all have unique fingerprints, that our red blood cells have a special shape, and more. You learned just how incredible the human body is.

By completing the activities in this book, you experimented and tried new things. These activities are what scientists do every day to learn more about the world around us. You've seen how engineers, artists, and inventors use different tools to understand the human body. You've explored the different systems that work together inside your body to get different jobs done.

You can come back and try the experiments again. Flip back to your favorite activities and look at the Try This! section for ideas on how to change them up!

You can keep learning to find out even more amazing things. See page 114 for some amazing resources to continue your STEAM adventures.

GLOSSARY

ABDOMEN: the part of your body between your chest and pelvis

ANATOMY: the study of the structures of living things

BICONCAVE DISC: the special shape of red blood cells

BINOCULAR VISION: using two eyes with overlapping fields of view, which allows you to know how far away something is

BONE MARROW: the soft, sponge-like tissue at the center of most bones. Bone marrow produces blood cells.

CELL: the smallest unit that can live on its own. Cells make up all living organisms and the tissues of the body.

CELL MEMBRANE: a film that separates the inside of a cell from the outside of a cell. Different cell membranes allow different things to pass through them.

CHEMICAL ELEMENTS: pure substances that are made from a single atom

CHEMISTRY: the science of chemical elements and compounds

CIRCULATORY SYSTEM: the system that carries blood around the body, which includes the heart and blood vessels

DIGESTIVE SYSTEM: the system that helps us process food and extract energy from it

DNA: deoxyribonucleic acid, the material that carries all the information about how a living thing will look and function

ENGINEERING: the science of creating and building things using math and science

ENZYME: a substance that speeds up biochemical reactions. Enzymes can build up or break down other molecules.

EVAPORATE: to turn from a liquid to a gas

IRIS: the colored part of your eye. The iris contains muscles that help the pupil get bigger or smaller.

JOINTS: places in your body where your bones meet

LUNG CAPACITY: the amount of air that goes in and out of our lungs

LYMPH: a clear fluid that contains white blood cells. Lymph helps clean some tissues in the body and drains into the bloodstream.

MICROSCOPE: a tool used to look at objects (like cells) that are too small to be seen with the naked eye.

MUSCLES: soft tissues that control all movement in your body, both voluntary (like moving your arm) or involuntary (like your heartbeat)

NEURON: a nerve cell that carries electrical impulses

OBSERVATIONS: what we see when we are doing an experiment

OPPOSABLE THUMB: a thumb that can touch the fingers of the same hand, allowing us to grasp things

ORGAN: a group of tissues in a living organism that has a specific form and function

ORGAN SYSTEM: a group of one or more organs that work together to do one or more jobs

OSMOSIS: the movement of water through a semi-permeable membrane

PAPILLAE: the little bumps on the top of the tongue and around the mouth that contain taste buds

PHYSICS: the science that deals with matter, energy, motion, and force

PHYSIOLOGY: the study of the processes and activities that keep things alive

PROTEIN: the substance that builds, maintains, and replaces the tissues in your body

PUPIL: the black center of your eye through which the light enters

RESPIRATORY SYSTEM: the system that allows us to breathe. We breath in oxygen and breath out carbon dioxide.

SCIENCE: the study of the world around us. Scientists learn about their subject by observing, describing, and experimenting.

SKELETAL SYSTEM: all the bones in the human body. The skeletal system helps us move and keep our body upright.

STATES OF MATTER: the forms in which matter can exist. There are four states of matter: solid, liquid, gas, and plasma.

TISSUES: groups of cells that work together to do a job in the body

RESOURCES

Here's a list of some great places on the web to learn more about the human body and the wonderful world of STEAM. Ask an adult to help you access these sites.

Go Science Kids:
gosciencekids.com/steam-activities-kids

Left Brain Craft Brain:
leftbraincraftbrain.com/28-days-of-stem -activities-and-steam-activities-for-kids

Our Family Code:
ourfamilycode.com

Science Sparks:
science-sparks.com

STEAM Powered Family:
steampoweredfamily.com

The STEM Laboratory:
thestemlaboratory.com/stem-activities -for-kids

INDEX

ABOUT THE AUTHOR

Dr. Orlena trained as a pediatric doctor. She teaches moms and their families to lead healthy lives in a way that is easy and fun. Check out her podcast, *Fit and Fabulous at 40 and Beyond*, and her book, *Building Simple Habits to a Healthy Me*.

Galen and Dante were 13 and 11 when they helped Dr. Orlena write this book. They love math, science, and playing computer games, so working with their mom on this book was great fun for them.

Printed in the USA
CPSIA information can be obtained
at www.ICGtesting.com
CBHW041725160424
6994CB00010B/161